The Unofficial Power Pressure Cooker XL®Cookbook

JACKIE WHITE

Unofficial Power Pressure Cooker XL®Cookbook

© 2016 by Cooking With A Foodie Press. All rights reserved.

All images licensed by Shutterstock:

Fanfo p. 77 | Liliya Kandrashevich p. 186 | Dream79 p. 101 | gkrphoto p. 71 | cobraphotography p. 96 | margouillat photo p. 183 | Karl Allgaeuer p. 109 | Africa Studio p. 26 | VICUSCHKA p. 18 | Dasha Petrenko p. 181 | JoannaTkaczuk p. 172 | Tatiana Vorona p. 127 | Foodio p. 152 | Elena Veselova p. 166 | Shaiith p. 156 | zkruger p. 193 | vanillaechoes p. 115 | marco mayer p. 161 | Elena Shashkina p. 119 | Bochkarev Photography p. 66 | stockcreations p. 75 | istetiana p. 84 | Bochkarev Photography p. 142 | ma23ma23 p. 191

Join Our FREE Cookbook Club

Why should you join?

- ⊘ Get new books we publish for free
- ⊘ Get huge discounts on new products we promote
- ⊘ Get recipes, secrets and techniques straight from the pros to your inbox
- ⊘ Get access to our convenient kitchen guides

SIGN UP AT COOKINGWITHAFOODIE.COM

Table of Contents

PRESSURE COOKING BASICS

A bit of history

The modern pressure cooking pot is the result of the evolution of a series of historical scientific experiments.

This tightly heated-valve-steam-machine was once the human hallmark of engineering – the forefather of the cylinder-engine and the heart of our locomotives and ships.

It was a Frenchman (of course!) who converted all our high-pressure and heat theories into one experiment: the Bone Digester. In 1682, Denys Papin brought his giant machine to the Royal Society in London and mesmerized scientists with meat bones as soft as gelatin.

Manufactured in France in the late 1600s, pressure cookers were first available only in factories, for the industrial clans, the academicals, the scientists and adventurers. But since the last century, it has become part of the daily family life from every cultural background – the poor and the rich, the lazy and the healthy, the gourmet and newbie chefs.

Today it can sit safely in your kitchens and boil delicious sauces and broths in the most efficient way, effortlessly reducing hard ingredients down to super nutritious stews and soups.

Gentle Reminder:

Remember: this book is not a replacement for your Power Pressure Cooker XL®'s User Guide. Please check the literature provided by the manufacturer before using this machine.

Why should you own an electric pressure cooker?

For those with a large family and little time, the **Power Pressure Cooker XL®** is the best kitchen acquisition of the year - hands down. If you don't know how to cook, and if you are excited about the overwhelming cooking shows and recipes that pop up on the Internet and TV every minute, now is the moment to join the foodies and start preparing your own meals.

The plug-and-play versatility of this cooker even makes it perfect for cabins, getaway houses and beach bungalows. And the possibilities of the digital timer can transform your kitchen into a little factory of not just entire meals, but also sauces, soups and stews.

Benefits & advantages

This is an advanced cooking machine with dozens of applications. There's much more to it than just cooking. You could easily lose yourself and dedicate an entire lifetime to the perfection of a single high-pressure cooked dish. Or you can keep it on a corner and just use it for a very specific task, like canning or sterilizing. But if you want six of the most heard advantages of such a cooker, here they are:

1. Save Time

Do you like cooking for hours and hours? I bet you don't! That's where the amazing Power Pressure Cooker XL® comes in handy. Now you don't need to stand for hours and hours staring through the glass door of your oven watching over your steak or preparing a smoker with dozens of different wood chips, or, well, you got the idea. This machine is fast, and you will understand the nitty-gritties in the next chapters, as you read about the wonders of the high pressure world. Here is a quick example: a vegetable stock requires at least 2 hours in a regular stovetop pot to be made. But with the **Power Pressure Cooker XL®**, it's done in 30 minutes.

2. Easy to Cook and Clean

Enough of the complex food making and extended hours of cleaning. With this machine you don't need to puzzle around the kitchen with pots, pans, boilers, covers, spoons, forks or knives. No. Here, all you need is what comes in the box. And what is it? A pot and a ladle. Who could imagine that it is possible to cook incredible meals with such few items? This machine is the classic one-pot meal maker and the main advantage is that now you have more time to be with you family.

3. The Healthy Side

When you cook food under high pressure, the vitamins and the nutrients remain in the food for longer periods of time. Thanks to the reduced amount of time and water, all those amazing juices from the food stay together, making the ingredients well cooked, yet tasty and healthy. There are several studies out there proving that high-pressure cookers can retain from 90% to 95% of nutrients, almost double the amount when compared to the regular boiling process. That means your frozen or conserved foods will be also tasty after several days. And that's exactly what your family needs.

4. Save Energy

The good thing about cooking under high pressure is that you end up using less energy when compared to regular cooking pots. And when you use less energy, you save the planet and keep more money in your bank account. That's one of the best advantages of this machine – it makes you frugal and ecologically savvy at the same time.

5. Design

Just look at this beautiful and sturdy machine. It looks like you could cook a whole chicken in it. (Actually, that's the first recipe in our book!) Some people like it so much they bring the machine to the table and serve the meal directly from it. Others like to just stare at it ad nauseam until the clean and slick exterior design sparks an unexpected inspiration for lunch.

6. Preserving

Canning is the new American mania. And while there's a lot of discussion in the blogs regarding whether you can do it in a pressure cooker, the manufacturer claims it's perfect for it. We don't recommend you to commercialize your canning experiments, but you are free to test it for yourself and learn how food safety regulations work under your own standards.

Safety

The classic pressure cooking pots were noisy machines, loudly pumping out steam and spitting water everywhere. But now, the third generation American dream has transformed the old-school pressure cooker into the **Power Pressure Cooker XL®**. A multi-function cooking machine with timer, stir-browning mode and a sturdy lid with extra safety features. No more messy kitchens in 2016. We are in the spaceship era of cooking now.

Built-in Safety Features

1. Lid Safety Device: it protects the lid from opening until all the pressure is released.

2. Pressure and Temperature Sensor Controls: it maintains heat and pressure, and automatically deactivates the power supply when necessary.

3. Backup Release Valve: in case of malfunction of the Lid Safety Device, this feature kicks in and releases the built in pressure.

4. Clog Resistance: it prevents food from blocking the steam.

5. Spring Load: in case of emergencies, the bottom of the machine lowers the pot and the Rubber Gasket, enabling the steam and the pressure to escape.

6. Temperature Cut-Off: once the temperature rises beyond limit, the power supply is automatically cut off.

STOVETOP VS. ELECTRIC PRESSURE COOKERS

Different in every way from a conventional stovetop pressure pot, the **Power Pressure Cooker XL®** doesn't require constant attention. This machine was designed with an electronic panel that controls both the heating and the cooking time. This feature makes it safer and easier for the chef to go on with the daily routine, preparing other dishes, juggling fruits and vegetables around the kitchen (this is perfect for this new ADD generation that can't concentrate in one place for very long).

While you go cook something else, the **Power Pressure Cooker XL®** works throughout a preset number of minutes and turns the heat down automatically, settling into WARM-UP mode. The steam will then leave the pot gradually and naturally.

The stovetop models are also great tools. But the **Power Pressure Cooker XL®**sets itself in a different category, making a great contender against rice cookers and electric crock pots. If you are planning on buying any of those machines, consider the advantages of the high-pressure cooker.

THE ANATOMY OF APRESSURE COOKER

Are you ready for some science? A Rubber Ribbon Gasket controls the air between the pot and lid, holding the vapor and the water from the ingredients under pressure inside the machine. All down to 14 pounds per square inch max.

Meanwhile, the steel pot seals in the steam, pressuring the liquids and the solids down, lowering the water boiling point and keeping all the deliciousness from escaping. This reduces the regular cooking time and keeps the nutrients fresh for long periods of time.

The pressure is secured by the vacuum force created by the heat, making it humanly impossible to be opened while in full pressure.But please, don't try to prove science wrong and mess around with the lid while the cooker is in use.

The machine automatically lowers the heat to WARM mode once the preset cooking time is reached. The pot can keep your food hot for up to 4 hours. It's perfect for those stews that should last for long periods of time, like in a ski cabin or a family party that continues throughout the day.

Quick release vs. natural release

Once the preset time is reached, you can let the steam escape naturally or use the quick release method. Don't worry too much about which one to use for now. Every recipe in this book will guide you to the best method.

In any case, always be careful and soak up the residual steam by gently placing a clean cloth over the PRESSURE VALVE before opening it.

The quick release

The quick release is the most used method in this book. Simply turn the PRESSURE VALVE carefully with a kitchen glove or towel and open the lid. In this way, the high-pressured steam will be abruptly released and the food is immediately ready for serving. It's perfect for those fast cooking meals like seafood or steamed vegetables.

The natural release

To let the steam come out naturally all you need to do is... nothing! Yes, that's how this amazing machine works. As soon as the preset time is reached, make sure the power is shut off and in 5 to 20 minutes the vapor will be gone from the pot. You can then just open the PRESSURE VALVE and the lid. This method is recommended for recipes that require a few extra minutes of cooking (like bone stews) and for those recipes with ingredients that generate high amounts of foam and froth.

> *Watch out for high-density foods that create foam and frost: dry grains like lentils, beans, chickpeas, fresh roots like carrots or celery, starchy vegetables like potato, manioc, dairy products and any type of pasta and/or byproducts of flour.*

Which method should I use, after all?

Some people like to shorten the cooking time and use the natural release method to cook it further. Others prefer to cook the meal thoroughly and then use the quick release method to save time. There's nothing wrong with any of those styles. As soon as you become comfortable with high-pressure cooking, you will be able to experiment with it.

High pressure vs low pressure

The **Power Pressure Cooker XL®**cooks in 3 different pressure settings. Most of the dishes in this book can be done in the medium pressure.

To quickly cook bone broths and meat stews, the high-pressure setting is recommended.

But depending on the natural consistency of some of the ingredients you cook, you might want to take the pressure down a notch. Soft vegetables, seafood and fish are some examples of ingredients that require low pressure and a short cooking time.

Don't worry, we will guide you through which button to press accordingly to each ingredient and desired effect.

Cooking from frozen

Don't be ashamed of not using fresh foods every day. We know that sometimes you just need to fix a fast meal for your family, so why not? But here is quick reminder: frozen food stores large quantities of water. Be aware of this when adapting recipes to frozen vegetables, fruits or stocks. You might want to reduce the amount of additional water/stock to avoid overflowing. You could also simply add to the cooking time. To be safe, stir-fry/sauté the frozen ingredients before adding the water/stock and closing the lid for high pressure.

HOW TO ADJUST RECIPES FOR THE POWER PRESSURE COOKER XL®

You can cook any classic non-pressure recipe in the **Power Pressure Cooker XL®**. Every recipe that asks for braising, stirring, sautéing and boiling can be done here, with one tool. As soon as you start cooking with it, you will be more and more comfortable with experimenting. So do it! Steal (or borrow) the old cookbooks from your grandma and introduce your family to a revolution in the kitchen. Just be aware of some details:

Liquids. Thanks to the concentrated steam, you will need less water or stock when cooking with pressure. The rule of thumb is to add the liquid just above the minimum recommended (1/4 of the pot) and always below the maximum recommended (2/3 of the pot).

Timing. Remember: the high pressure speeds up the cooking. You might need only 1/3 of the time recommended by the traditional stovetop low-pressure recipes. Check out our tables for the cooking times for each different ingredient and calculate it yourself.

Altitude. The atmospheric pressure of the city you live can influence the cooking time drastically. All the recipes are made for sea level, but those of you cooking well above 6.000 feet should consider at least 5% longer cooking times. Depending on your ingredients being rich in water, the cooking time could be raised by 30%. Keep an eye out for dry foods like those persistent potatoes, beetroots and maniocs that never get done in time.

COOKING GUIDES

If you have no idea about planning your meals, this chapter is for you. The **Power Pressure Cooker XL®**can change your routine drastically. By being able to prepare and store large quantities of food, your family meals can now be done faster and be planned well in advance.

Family meal plan

Finding out your family's favorite dishes.

There's no better way to start a meal plan. Ask each member of your family for their favorite ingredients and keep a weekly/monthly track of the desired dishes.

Cooking and freezing.

Now that you can easily batch cook, you can even plan your homemade frozen meals. Start with dishes that usually require long cooking times (beans and chickpeas, for example). But be wise and do the same with your family's favorite meals.

Watch out for special events.

Some dates require special meal planning. But don't stress out at the last minute. Keep track of your family's most important events and cook in advance.

Weekly meal example.

Use the following schedule as a rough example. Adapt ingredients to your own taste, get the feedback from your family and friends to make a sequence of perfect meals that will make everyone proud of eating at home.

MONDAY

BREAKFAST

Banana rice pudding, served with fresh fruit juice, a slice of bread with jam/butter.

LUNCH

Lemongrass Chicken Coconut, served with rice and steamed vegetables.

DINNER

Tomato Soup, served with bread and salad.

TUESDAY

BREAKFAST

Apple sauce and fruit salad, served with fresh fruit juice, a slice of bread with jam/butter.

LUNCH

Mongolian Beef, served with noodles and salad.

DINNER

Coconut Curry Fish, served with rice and steamed vegetables.

WEDNESDAY

BREAKFAST

Egg Omelet, served with fresh fruit juice and a slice of bread with jam/butter.

LUNCH

Mediterranean Fish, served with bread and salad.

DINNER

Pumpkin soup, served with bread and vegetable antipasti.

THURSDAY

BREAKFAST

Yogurt, granola and fruit salad, served with fresh fruit juice, bread, and jam/butter.

LUNCH

Carrot Soup, served with Mashed Sweet Potatoes and steamed vegetables.

DINNER

Lemon Herb Chicken, served with noodles and salad.

BREAKFAST

Creamy Scrambled Eggs, served with fresh fruit juice and slice of bread with jam/butter.

LUNCH

Red Pepper Soup, served with Polenta and salad.

DINNER

Beef Stew, served with bread and salad.

SATURDAY

BREAKFAST

Fruit Marmalade, granola and fruit salad, served with fresh fruit juice, bread with jam/butter.

LUNCH

Whole Chicken, served with mashed potatoes and salad.

DINNER

Vegetable Broth Soup, served with bread and steamed vegetables.

SUNDAY

BREAKFAST

Fruit Marmalade, served with pancakes, fresh fruit juice and slice of bread with jam/butter.

LUNCH

Mexican Beef, served with tortillas, guacamole and salad.

DINNER

Mushroom Barley Soup, served with bread and salad.

PANTRY STOCKING GUIDE

Don't be ashamed if you don't know how to prepare your ingredients for cooking. Many of them can be a mystery to any of us. This seems more relevant nowadays considering that we can have so many exotic fruits and vegetables from all over the world in our local supermarkets (how does one even eat Kumquat?!).

Here we explain how to deal with each the most commonly used ingredients mentioned in the recipes. Many of them are worth buying in bulk. To get the best out of the **Power Pressure Cooker XL®**, we recommend that you cook them as fresh as possible and preserving the leftovers immediately.

The following is a list of the most commonly used ingredients in this book. Use it as a guide for your shopping list.

Salt: we recommend sea salt or kosher for meats. Regular refined salt works great for soups and stews.

Pepper: black and red pepper seasoning works great for almost everything. Try a sweet chili pepper seasoning when cooking Mexican food.

Chicken (breast, wings, legs): remove the bones and the skin when desired. Give it a good rinse with water before cooking. Let it soak in a marinade and spices for a delicious upgrade in taste and aroma.

Garlic: fresh or dry, always peel it before cooking.

Onions: always peel them before cooking. Replace with spring onions or leeks for a pleasant change in taste.

Carrots: always peel them before cooking.

Rice (arborio, jasmine, risotto): rinsing rise is usually a good way to get rid of unwanted substances that sometimes sneak into rice bags.

Beef (steak, ribs, marrow bones): ask your butcher for the right cut before shopping. Aim for the freshest meats.

Cooking oil (olive, coconut, peanut, soy, sunflower): extremely necessary for sautéing, we recommend olive for western cuisine and peanut for Asian dishes.

Tomatoes: seed and peel them for tomato based sauces. Just give it a good wash for anything else. Use the canned version if you have no time to lose.

Fruit salad (apple, orange, pineapple, strawberry, banana): peel off the harsh fruits like pineapple and banana before eating them. Remove seeds and core of apples, pears, and oranges.

Butter: great replacement for oils. Use it for sautéing meats and mushrooms. Add a spoonful to rice and lentils.

Pork (shoulder, roast, ribs): ask your butcher for the right cut before shopping. Aim for the freshest meats.

Potatoes: peel them when desired.

Sweet potatoes: peel them when desired.

Herbs (thyme, rosemary, oregano, parsley, bay leaf, cilantro, coriander, marjoram, sage, basil): thyme and oregano are great with vegetables. Rosemary goes brilliantly with pork and potatoes. Cilantro and coriander are a must on Latin-American dishes. Marjoram sits perfectly with fish.

Lemon: a little dash is enough to enhance your dish, but too much will make it sour. So watch out and always add it close to the final steps of cooking.

Coconut milk: use the unsweetened version for savory dishes.

Cheese (parmesan, ricotta, mozzarella): we recommend these but you are free to search and learn about the hundreds types of cheeses and experiment with your discoveries.

Eggplant: wash them well before cooking.

Beetroot: always wash and peel them off before cooking.

Swiss Chard: wash and rinse it before cooking. It usually needs just a few minutes of heat, so better add them at the end.

Kale: wash and rinse them before cooking.

Turnips: wash and scrub them before cooking. Remove greens if desired.

Celery: remove bruises and dice them in tiny pieces for sautéing.

Bell Pepper: red, green or yellow, always seed them before cooking. Dice them in tiny pieces for sautéing.

Ginger: dry or fresh, always peel them before cooking.

Dry white wine (Riesling, Sauvignon Blanc, Chardonnay): use it for deglazing chicken, seafood, fish, or vegetables.

Dry red wine (Cabernet Sauvignon, Merlot, Pinot Noir): use it for deglazing red meats and vegetables.

Whisky (single malt, bourbon): it goes great with meat, BBQ sauce and sweet-citrus fruits.

Dry Sherry: great for deglazing meats, vegetables and cream.

Olives: black or green, seed them to avoid surprises.

Corn: in a cob or in a can, always remove the silk exterior before cooking.

Pasta (penne, tortellini, fusilli): dry or fresh, look for the shape that makes you happiest.

Chocolate: use at least 60% cacao for a more bitter and adult palate.

Beans (black, pinto, white, lentils, chickpeas): wash and rinse them before cooking. Let them soak in broth, marinade or water to reduce the cooking time.

Fish (cod, tuna, salmon): talk to your butcher before buying. Ask him to gut and clean the fish of bones. Peel off skin if desired. Always aim for the freshest fish.

Broccoli, Cauliflower: frozen or fresh, rinse it with water and vinegar to remove debris in between the florets.

Milk: whole or 2% fat, watch out for frost and foam while cooking with it under pressure.

Cabbage: green or purple, choose the color you like the most and mix and match with other greens to make a great salad.

Seafood (clams, shrimps, mussels): always wash, rinse and scrub to remove debris. Peel off skin, shells, and veins when desired.

Lemongrass: dry or fresh, discard the outer stalks. It's a must in many Asian dishes.

Flour (wheat, corn, barley): there are hundreds of types of flour out there. Use it for baking and for thickening soups and stews.

Vinegar (apple cider, red/white wine, balsamic): we recommend apple cider and dry red vinegar for meat and vegetables. Use dry white for fish and seafood.

Buttersquash: always seed them and peel them before cooking.

Cereal (granola mix, corn, oatmeal): great breakfast ingredient, choose the one your family loves the most.

Vanilla: dry or fresh, a few spoons can change a dessert forever.

Mushroom: always scrub and wash them before cooking.

Spinach: frozen or fresh, always rinse with water to remove debris.

Yogurt: aim for whole yogurt when creating your own culture. Use Greek or 2% fat for sauces.

Avocado: smash it with salt and lemon to create your own guacamole.

Egg: always aim for the freshest.

Zucchini: just give it a good clean before cooking.

Worcestershire sauce: find your favorite brand and stick to it.

Peanut: dry or in butter form, use the unsweetened kind for savory dishes.

Spices (curry, turmeric, paprika, saffron, vanilla): an endless world of possibilities, learn their tastes and aromas and manage your own dosage.

SPECIFIC INGREDIENT & COOKING TIMES GUIDE

In the following pages you will find the usual cooking times for different foods that cook perfectly under pressure. This is ideal for cooking in bulk and freezing. You don't need to add any spices or salt at this point. It's much easier for you to add additional flavors when preparing frozen food. You could cook and freeze a bunch of beans for example, and add garlic, onions and salt just at the last minute, after you defrost it.

Be aware that mixing extra ingredients may add a few minutes to the cooking time. Always use CANNING/PRESERVING to cook meals with high heat and high pressure, and adjust time accordingly to each ingredient. Use the quick release method unless the ingredient may be generating too much foam and froth.

Vegetables

The size, the ripeness, the health, and the freshness of vegetables can influence the cooking time. The following table estimates the necessary time for cooking the most abundant leeks, greens, legumes and roots.

Ingredient (½ of the pot and at least ¼ of water/stock)	Cooking Time (in minutes)
Artichoke hearts	6 to 11
Asparagus	2 to 4
Beets	15 to 25
Beet greens	2 to 3
Bell peppers	2 to 5
Broccoli	5 to 8
Brussels sprouts	3 to 5
Cabbage, red, or white	5 to 8
Carrots	2 to 8
Cauliflower	2 to 4
Celery	2 to 4
Chestnuts	7 to 10
Corn kernels	2
Corn on the cob	3 to 7
Endives / escarole	2
Eggplant (aubergine)	2 to 4
Fennel bulb	2 to 4

Green beans	2 to 4
Kale	2 to 4
Kohlrabi (German turnip)	5 to 8
Kohlrabi	2 to 4
Leeks	2 to 4
Okra	2 to 4
Onions	2 to 7
Parsnips	2 to 8
Peas	2 to 3
Potatoes	5 to 10
Pumpkin	2 to 5
Spinach	1 to 3
Squash, butternut	3 to 5
Sweet potato	5 to 10
Tomatoes	2 to 3
Turnips	2 to 6
Yellow beans (wax beans)	2 to 4
Zucchini	2 to 3

Fruits

Remove the seeds and the skin when desired. Pressure cooked fruits make great jellies and jams, cakes and candies, desserts in general. Replace the water/stock with fruit juice to add a second layer of flavor.

Ingredient (½ of the pot and at least ¼ of water/juice)	Cooking Times (in minutes)
Apples	3 to 8
Apricots, dried	5
Apricots, fresh	3
Banana	1
Blueberries	1
Cherries	1
Cranberries	3 to 5

Dates	10
Figs	6 to 10
Grapes	1
Lemons	2
Oranges	2
Peaches	4
Pears	3 to 8
Pineapple (slices)	6
Plums	1
Prunes	5
Raisins	5
Raspberries	1
Strawberries	1

Cereals, Beans, Dry Foods

The trick with dry foods is to leave them soaking in water overnight. Stock, juice, or any kind of sauce also works. It reduces the cooking time and adds amazing flavors to the dish. And remember: letting the pressure escape naturally can compensate for some of the cooking time. Keep an eye out for the ingredients cooking even after the machine is completely shut off.

Ingredient (½ of the pot and at least ¼ of water/stock)	Cooking Times After Soaked (in minutes)	Cooking Times Non-Soaked (in minutes)
Beans (black)	5 to 10	8 to 28
Beans (lima)	4. 8	12 to 20
Beans (pinto)	4. 8	22 to 28
Beans, (red kidney)	10 to 14	20 to 28
Beans, (beige)	10 to 14	30 to 35
Beans, (white kidney)	8 to 12	30 to 40
Chickpeas	14 to 20	30 to 45
Lentils, green	5 to 10	10 to 15
Lentils, red, split	5 to 8	8 to 12
Peas, split, green or yellow	8 to 10	10 to 20
Peas, dried, whole	10 to 14	10 to 20
Peanuts	10 to 15	15 to 30

Meats

Many aspects can influence the cooking time of meat. The origin, the size of the bones, the amount of fat, the freshness of the cuts, the quality of the food the animal was eating. Be on the safe side and let them cook until as tender as possible.

Remember: the following tables do not consider sauté/browning the meat beforehand. Depending on the cut, the sauté/stir-frying process could add at least 20 more minutes to the total cooking time.

Beef

Ingredient (½ of the pot and at least ¼ of water/stock)	Cooking Times (in minutes)
Beef Brisket	45 to 70
Beef Steak	30 to 35
Beef Ground	5 to 8
Beef Heart	50 to 80
Beef Kidney	8 to 12
Beef Liver	5 to 8
Beef Neck Bones	40 to 50
Beef Oxtails	40 to 50
Beef Short ribs	20 to 25
Beef Tongue	75 to 95

Poultry

Ingredient (½ of the pot and at least ¼ of water/stock)	Cooking Times (in minutes)
Chicken Boneless Strips	3 to 5
Chicken Breasts	6 to 8
Chicken Breasts Boneless	5 to 8
Chicken Giblets (Neck, bones and insides)	25 to 30
	2 to 4
Chicken Livers	4 - 5
Chicken Ground	7 to 8
Chicken Legs	5 - 6
Chicken Legs Boneless	4 - 5
Chicken Wings	20 to 25
Chicken Whole (3 - 4 lbs)	5 - 6
Eggs Hard-Boiled	2 to 3
Eggs Poached	8 to 10
Duck Boneless Strips	25 to 35
Duck Whole (3 - 4 lbs)	20 to 25
Turkey Breast	20 to 22
Turkey Breast Boneless	25 to 30
Turkey Giblets (Neck, bones and insides)	8 to 10
	12 to 15
Turkey Ground	10 to 15
Turkey Thigh	40 to 45
Turkey Thigh Boneless	
Turkey Whole (10-12 lbs)	

Pork

Ingredient (½ of the pot and at least ¼ of water/stock)	Cooking Times (in minutes)
Pork Chops	6 to 10
Pork Loin	25 to 40
Pork Feet	30 to 40
Pork Spareribs	10 to 15
Pork Baby Back Ribs	12 to 15
Pork Roasts	30 to 40
Pork Sausage	8 to 10
Pork Shanks	35 to 40
Pork Shoulder	35 to 45
Ham Uncooked Shanks	40 to 50
Ham Fully Cooked Shanks	20 to 40

Others

Ingredient (½ of the pot and at least ¼ of water/stock)	Cooking Times (in minutes)
Lamb Breast	35 to 45
Lamb Chops	10 to 15
Lamb Riblets	6 to 10
Lamb Leg (3 lbs.)	20 to 25
Lamb Neck/Shoulder (3 to 6 lbs)	25 to 30
Lamb Shanks	20 to 30
Lamb Steak	8 to 10
Veal Leg (3 - 4 lbs)	50 to 70
Veal Roast (3 - 4 lbs)	40 to 50
Veal Shanks	20 to 30
Rabbit Whole	10 to 20
Goat Chops	30 to 40

THE ULTIMATE POWER PRESSURE COOKER XL® GUIDE

Fear not, technophobes! The **Power Pressure Cooker XL®** has managed to put complex cooking combinations in a few program buttons. Check out what each one of them can do:

Program Buttons	Default Time	Temperature F°	Pressure (Psi)	Description
Delay Timer	N / A	N / A	N / A	Use it for programming your meals.
Canning / Preserving	10 mins	241	12	High-pressure and high heat. Use it also for stocks and broths.
Soup / Stew	10 mins	228	7.2	Medium-pressure setting with medium heat.
Slow Cook	2 hrs	174-199	<4.3	Low-pressure with low heat.
Rice / Risotto	6 min	228	7.2	Medium-pressure with low heat.
Beans / Lentils	5 mins	228	7.2	Medium-pressure with low heat.
Fish / Veg. / Steam	2 mins	228	7.2	Medium-pressure with low heat.
Meat / Chicken	15 mins	228	7.2	Medium-pressure with low heat.
Time Adjustment	10 mins	N / A	N / A	Your best friend in this machine. Use it to adapt the recipe times.
Cancel / Keep Warm	N / A	N / A	N / A	It cancels last program but keeps the pot warm.

Using the Power Pressure Cooker XL®

It's time to put your chef hat on. Basically, there are two ways of cooking with this machine. Every recipe in this book will guide you through the basic steps. Learn those techniques if you want to impress friends and family and create your very own recipe from scratch.

Without sautéing

For simple stews and light-colored broths, you just add the ingredients in the pot together with the water or broth. Give it a good mix. You then choose the desired Program/Time, close the lid, lock the seal, and wait for the miracle to happen. This method is great for cooking recipes quickly, especially the ones without meat.

Sauté/stir-fry mode

This method browns the dish by initially frying the ingredients in fat or oil. It adds beautiful flavors, aromatics and colors to your recipes and it only takes a few additional minutes when it comes to vegetables. Meats are a bit tougher to brown, so you might be looking at 5 to 20 minutes of sautéing here.

First, choose the desired program and wait for the oil or butter to heat up. Add the ingredients slowly while stirring. Once your dish looks brown and caramelized, add the water/stock, the remaining ingredients, and stir it well. Master the art of adding the ingredients gradually, observing the cooking time of each type of food. You can then close the lid, lock-up the seal, and let the pressure do the work.

Basic Sauté Ingredients
Oils (olive, sunflower, soy, peanut, coconut).
Fat (butter, ghee, lard, tallow)
Garlic.
Onions.
Peppers.
Celery.
Spring-onions.
Carrots.
Mushrooms.
Herbs (thyme, oregano, basil, chives, dill, sage, marjoram)

Deglazing

This is a fancy name for the technique of balancing dry and wet ingredients while sautéing. Slowly pour in water, broth, wine or cognac over the ingredients in the hot pot for a quick aromatic effect. The alcohol from the booze instantly evaporates and all that's left is a delicious and refined fermented juice taste.

Scorching

The food residue that keeps getting attached to the bottom of the pot is your friend. Learn to scoop it out as the pot heats up fast. The fat cooks certain ingredients way too quickly (i'm looking at you garlic!), so watch out and don't leave the pot while sautéing/scorching. Mix it with your deglazing techniques and soon you will be mastering the art of never burning a dish.

CLEANING GUIDE

The **Power Pressure Cooker XL®** must be cleaned after each use. But first you must wait for it to cool down. Never, I repeat, never clean it while the machine is hot.

1.Unplug unit and allow it to cool off completely.

2. Remove the Pressure Valve and clean the opening with a pin to remove any blockage that might have occurred during the cooking process.

3. The Removable Cooking Pot and Lid are immersible for cleaning. Rinse they under hot running water. Use a mild liquid detergent and a soft cloth, sponge or nylon scrubber for cleaning. Do not use abrasive powders, bicarbonate of soda or bleach. Do not use scouring pads.

4. When cleaning the Lid, the Rubber Gasket must be removed and washed separately with a sponge or soft cloth and warm, soapy water.

5. Wipe the base with a soft, damp cloth or sponge. DO NOT IMMERSE BASE IN WATER.

6. Always check that the Pressure Valve, the Float Valve and the Rubber Gasket are in good working order and debris free.

PRESSURE COOKER ACCESSORIES

This is what should come in the box. Check that everything is there before you start to cook.

Measuring Cup:

for recipes that require perfect measurement.

Ladle:

stirs up your food without damaging the inner pot.

Condensation Collector:

picks up the excess moisture from the channel on the back of the cooker.

Steamer Tray:

keeps the ingredients above the water for delicious steamed dishes. Use it also for canning.

DO'S AND DON'TS

1. Never deep fry in a pressure cooker.

2. Never touch the RELEASE VALVE while cooking.

3. Always check on the RUBBER GASKET before cooking.

4. Never cook without any liquid inside the pot.

5. Never try to open the lid while cooking.

REVIEWS

We reviewed hundreds of comments in Amazon and Google. But you know the internet, there's always a few trolls out there or someone paid by the company to write good things about them. We went ahead and compiled a list of the top pros and cons you will read about this machine.

Pros

- the sauté/stir-fry mode puts it ahead of the game for the products in the same price range.

- it's big. You can easily cook a one-pot meal for 5 to 8 people in one run.

- it has so many safety convenient features built into the model, it basically runs on autopilot.

Cons

- it requires basic knowledge (very basic) of cooking and what heat and pressure does to the ingredients.

- it's not possible to change the temperature so easily while sauté/stir frying. You will need to constantly cancel and start new programs if you enjoy juggling heat high and low while stir-frying.

- for safety reasons, the machine doesn't reach the full pressure of 15psi compared to classic stovetop pots.

Quotes

Check out some of the beautiful things the people are saying about the **Power Pressure Cooker XL®**.

"It's convenient, easy to use. Have made chicken twice and many jams. Love it! Easy to convert recipes to the Power Pressure Cooker XL®. Can't say enough about it. I highly recommend." Patty Q.

"This thing works perfectly fine. I mean I, a horrible cook, just made my first pot roast in about 40 minutes total (15 minutes of prep) and it came out amazing (according to my children)." Joey T.

"I was able to replace my crockpot, my rice steamer and my old pressure cooker with this awesome product!" Coleen M.

Concentrated Stock Bases.

Throughout this book, we will tell you to use broths and stocks to add flavor and aroma to the dishes but they take some time to prepare.

That's why you can also experiment with stock bases. They are sold in paste, gel, powder and liquid forms. With a few spoons, the water gets all the full flavors of vegetables, beef, chicken or fish. This little secret ingredient can save a chef from a miscalculated recipe or a family with a sudden appetite for supper.

Try to combine brands and forms until you create your own stock mixture. But watch out for the high amounts of salt/sodium - that's what keep those bases from spoiling.

You can also create your own base by boiling and reducing your broth to gelatin. You could even freeze or can your stocks for a prolonged shelf life. Whatever you choose to do, any of those options is better than just using plain water.

NUTRITIONAL INFORMATION

The nutritional content of your meals can vary drastically depending on the produce and season. The quality of the water also influences the taste and, of course, the quality of the meal.

From the freshness of the produce, the way the ingredients and how the animals are cultivated, it all affects the nutritional content and taste of the dish. Be sure you know where your food comes from and how it's produced.

Calories

For the following recipes, we can't really calculate the calorie information of your dish without seeing the ingredients you are using. But we can tell you already – every meat recipe in this book is also a high-calorie dish. We are talking about veal knees and sausage-seafood meals here. Without a doubt, a full portion will be quite caloric.

The Mediterranean trick is to reduce the quantities of the main dish and add healthy and fresh sides to the meals. This way everyone eats well and enough. And you get to save the leftovers for cakes, sauces and sandwiches.

If you are going through a special diet, talk to your doctor before cooking or eating any of our recipes for the first time.

Fat and oil

There's not a single deep fried, oil-cooked based recipe in this book. But all the stir-frying-sauté is done with a sizzle of vegetable oil or butter.

The meats and stews are fat and rich in nutrients. Some protein-maniacs drink cold bone broth in the morning like a juice. Now that's the original energy drink.

Sugar

With a few exceptions, the desserts in this book are definitely high in sugar. Be aware of the quantities and consider them as sauces and toppings, always serving small portions along with fresh fruits, cereals and/or dairy products like cream or yogurt.

As for the industrialized products, we provide the quantities of each ingredient, so you should be able to calculate the sugar yourself just by looking at the nutritional information table placed on the package/label.

Salt/Sodium

Every recipe in this book recommends you to salt and season to taste. If you follow a specially salted diet, please talk to your doctor before cooking and eating any of our recipes.

Be aware of the ready-made products and the canned pickled goods. They carry high amounts of sodium and other things that, well, who knows? For a clearer consciousness, try to always strain, clean, rinse or mix the industrialized goods with running water before adding them to the meals.

Quick tip: remember to taste the dishes before adding salt in layers with small pinches.

We provide the quantities of each ingredient, so you should be able to calculate the amount of sodium by yourself. Look at the nutritional information table placed on the package/label to learn more.

PRESSURE COOKING HACKS.

Who could imagine that a pressure cooker is so versatile? Once you are familiar with the**Power Pressure Cooker XL®**, you can start experimenting with those advanced techniques and catch up with the French.

1. Sous vide

In France they call it bain-marie. This is an excellent way to warm up baby food, desserts, sauces, and delicate ingredients that can be eaten directly from containers.

It's basically a hot water bath for your food – a technique that helps to retain valuable nutrients thanks to the oxygen-free environment.

Start by placing your meals tightly vacuum sealed in glass jars. We recommend you using four 16 oz glass jars on this machine at the same time. This way you can fit in manageable portions of food while cooking without loss of temperature or space.

In the case of meat steaks, place them into silicon bags with herbs and spices and vacuum-seal them. And avoid plastic bags which release several chemical additives when heated that you really don't want in your food.

The basic steps

1. Add the STEAMER TRAY to the pot and pour in enough water to cover ¼ of the pot.

2. Cover the food jars tightly with a lid and place them over the tray.

3. Close the pot lid and lock the PRESSURE VALVE.

4. Hit the FISH/VEG/STEAM button and wait for the pressure to do the work. Adjust time if necessary. Under high-pressure, it might take only 2 to 5 minutes to warm up your food. Look at our cooking time list/table of ingredients to have an idea of which PROGRAM to use.

5. Once done, release pressure by quick release method.

6. Remove jars carefully. Bring food to plates or bowls and serve.

2. Tied pressure cooking

This when you cook with a bowl or a cooking dish (of glass or ceramic) inside the main pot with water. It holds the same principles of canning, but thanks to the wide format of the dish, Tied Pressure Cooking transforms the boiling process into some sort of high-pressure baking.

Many dessert recipes work this way. You can always cover your dishes tightly with aluminium foil to keep the food steam from mixing up with the water steam. This accelerates the cooking process and holds the tastes and the aromas intact. We recommend 2 lbs baking bowls of high grade ceramic or glass for this specific machine.

3. Using broth instead of water

This is every chef's secret. Cook meat and vegetable stocks in advance and substitute it into the recipes that ask for water. Now instead of diluting the ingredients, you are adding concentrated flavor to the meal.

4. Storing ,eftovers

Don't throw everything away after cooking! Scraps from meat, bones and peels from vegetables and fruits can become great and rich stocks. Give them a good wash and try it out. You can also freeze the scraps until you accumulate a good amount and suddenly save yourself a few bucks with a delicious broth out of leftovers. Just remember that cooked food usually lasts from 3-4 days in the fridge and 1 to 4 months in the freezer (depending on the ingredients). Raw food can last almost double the time (always check first).

We compiled a list of great tips for keeping your leftovers fresh and tasty.

1. Try to keep packaged goods in their original package. Don't move them around boxes and wraps to reduce their exposure to different materials and they will last longer. The same works for meats, fruits and vegetables.

2. Aluminium foil, wax paper and food saver bags are your allies in the battle against spoilage. Use them for wrapping fruits, vegetables and cheese, reducing waste and saving space in your fridge.

3. Don't mix different vegetables or fruits in the same container. You can avoid undesired fermentation by keeping ingredients from reacting to each other.

4. Don't wash your produce before putting them in the fridge. The water can increase the chance of mold growth, so be wise and just wash fruits and vegetables before cooking.

5. Keep your produce in the fridge with perforated bags. To store greens and leaves in a airtight container is not a good idea as they need air circulation. Remember: that lower drawer from your fridge is the perfect produce space, so use it!

6. Warm leftovers need two hours of cooling off before moving to the fridge or freezer. Always keep them in airtight containers.

5. Canning

This is a traditional and easy technique for stocking fresh vegetables, fruits, soups, sauces and jams. Seems like everyone is doing it! It works by cooking the ingredients in a sealed jar with limited air contact. You can't compete with industry standards without vacuum sealing your jars and without the pasteurization process. So please don't market your preserved meals and watch out for the fabrication date before consumption.

There are two basic ways of canning:

Raw Packing

The process of canning fresh and unheated foods. Great for fresh fruits and vegetables.

Hot Packing

The process of canning foods that have been pre-cooked before packing them in jars. Great for jams and sauces.

Canning Tools

If you are serious about your canning, you will need some new accessories.

16 oz Canning Jars

You can fit four 16 oz jars in your **Power Pressure Cooker XL®.** Careful with the jars that have a ribbon gasket. They will trigger another vacuum system and you don't want that to happen. Cover them with aluminium foil instead or use the jars with a basic metal screw system.

Canning Tongs

A holder and lifter that allows you to handle the jars without directly touching them.

Steam Tray / Wire Rack

Surface that holds the jars just above the bottom of the pot.

The Basic-Steps

1. Fill the jars almost completely, leaving an inch or two of headspace. In case of raw fruits or vegetables, complete with water, stock or juice.

2. Lock the jars tightly with aluminium foil or a screw lid.

3. Place the jars over the rack and fill ¼ of the pot with water. With all the 4 jars, that's around 6 cups of water.

4. Select the Canning/Preserve program. Adjust the time as necessary.

5. Place lid on cooker, lock the PRESSURE SEAL, and bring up to pressure.

6. Once done, release pressure by quick release method.

7. Carefully lock the jars tightly with the proper lid immediately after cooking.

8. Let the jars cool off and store them in the fridge or freezer.

Ingredients/Cooking Time Table for Canning*

Food Item	Packing Conditions		Set Pressure to 80 kPa
	Style of Pack	Jar Size	Minutes
Asparagus	Hot & Raw	Pints	30
Beans (green)	Hot & Raw	Pints	20
Beans (lima, pinto, butter or soy)	Hot & Raw	Pints	40
Beets	Hot	Pints	30
Carrots	Hot & Raw	Pints	25
Corn, whole-kernel	Hot & Raw	Pints	55
Greens	Hot	Pints	70
Okra	Hot	Pints	25
Peas, Green or English	Hot & Raw	Pints	40
Potatoes, white	Hot	Pints	35
Meat Strips, Cubes, or Chunks	Hot or Raw	Pints	75
Ground or Chopped Meat	Hot or Raw	Pints	75
Poultry, without bones	Hot or Raw	Pints	75
Poultry, with bones	Hot or Raw	Pints	65

For processing times and methods for additional low acid foods, please refer to the National Center for Home Food Preservation (http://www.uga.edu/nchfp/): or your local county extension agent.

* provided by the manufacturer

Food Acidity

The lower the acidity of the food, the greater the potential for contamination. Many foods such as fruits and legumes are high in acid, where as meats, dairy products and sea foods have low acid levels. Be extra diligent when dealing with meat and eggs. Avoid overripe fruits and legumes. Always sterilize your tools, bowls and jars before using them.

Examples of High Acid Foods

Apples	Pickled Beets
Oranges	Cherries
Applesauce	Pineapple
Peaches	Cranberries
Apricots	Plums
Pears	Fruit Juices
Berries	Rhubarb

Examples of Low Acid Foods

Asparagus	Potatoes
Mushrooms	Hominy
Beans	Spinach
Okra	Meat
Beets	Winter Squash
Peas	Corn
Carrots	Seafood

Additional information

The efficiency of the Power Pressure Cooker XL® for canning and preserving food is scientifically accurate, but not approved by the USDA. Do your canning with extreme hygiene standards and at your own risk.

4. Sterilizing

Now here's a real hack – sterilizing with a pressure cooker. Use it with baby bottles, toys and pacifiers, glass jars, iron and steel blades, special cutlery sets, and even emergency surgery tools. These tips have been circulating around the Internet for years and now it's time for you to join the crowd with this technique.

Basic Steps

1. Place the WIRE RACK inside the pot and add enough water to cover the ¼ minimum necessary.

2. Place the items/utensils in need of sterilization over the rack. They should be completely rinsed, cleaned and scrub-washed beforehand. Make sure the items/utensils are not submerged in water.

3. Hit CANNING/PRESERVING followed by TIME ADJUSTMENT and correct time to 30 minutes.

4. Once done, let the pressure escape naturally.

5. Handle the sterilized tools with extreme caution by using tongs or tweezers.

6. Dry excess water with clean cloth.

Internal Cleaning

After using your pressure cooker for anything different than food, you better give it a good internal cleaning. Let the machine run with a few cups (3 or 4) of water for two minutes. The hot steam will wipe the residuals out of openings and vents, removing undesired tastes and aromas.

Additional Information

Regardless of its efficiency, the use of this machine for tool sterilization is not recommended by the manufacturer. As it states on the user's manual, the **Power Pressure Cooker XL®** should be only used with food. Do your sterilization with extreme hygiene standards and always at your own risk.

LETTER FROM THE AUTHOR

I grew up in the 90's with every grandma cooking in a prehistoric version of the **Power Pressure Cooker XL®**. They would stew hard fiber meats like veal and *ossobuco*, make unbelievable broths out of scraps, and cook delicious *dulce de leche* directly from condensed milk cans.

My mom would cook large amounts of beans and lentils. And by freezing a good part of it, we would be able to fix a quick and tasty meal out of the blue, saving both money and time.

The following dishes are a mixture of those classic family recipes with internet blogger hacks.

Watch out for the times and quantities, and be aware that every ingredient could have adverse reactions to high-pressure cooking. I've seen chickpeas require four hours of boiling under high-pressure to become soft. The same could happen to any starchy beans or lentils. Potatoes are infamous for being hard to boil. If you want to make meat out of bones, you have to be patient. Keep the soft leafy vegetables and seafoods under your watch before they disappear into the dish.

I hope you can take high-pressure cooking into practice and develop your own kitchen hacks. We need more inventors, cooks, farmers and recipe book writers to keep experimenting, discovering and sharing. Let's keep talking about delicious food and developing smart cooking techniques.

Happy cooking!

CHICKEN

Savory Whole Chicken

This five-ingredient whole chicken recipe is a staple if you want gourmet dinner served in less than 30 minutes. When the chicken is cooked, the meat comes right off the bone with a tasty, juicy sauce that you can turn into a lovely gravy once reduced along with some corn flour.

Serves: 4 - 6
Preparation Time: 5 minutes (chicken needs at least 1 hour soaked in spices)
Cooking Time: 25 minutes

INGREDIENTS:

Corn flour, to taste
Salt and pepper to taste
Olive oil to taste
(2 cups) Chicken broth
(2 lbs) Whole chicken

PREPARATION:

1. Place the chicken in a baking dish.

2. Coat the chicken evenly with salt and pepper to taste, including inside the meat.

3. Let it sit in the fridge for at least an hour before cooking.

COOKING STEPS:

1. Hit MEAT/CHICKEN followed by TIME ADJUSTMENT and correct time to 25 minutes.

2. Heat the oil and brown the chicken on all sides.

3. Add broth around chicken.

4. Place lid on cooker, lock the PRESSURE SEAL, and bring up to pressure.

5. Once done, release pressure by quick release method.

6. Bring chicken to a platter and serve with the accumulated sauce, mashed potatoes or polenta.

Chicken Jardinière

Now that's a deliciously fast chicken recipe. The vegetables and the meat will merge into one tasty garden of smells and colors, hence the name Jardinière. It goes great with rice and potatoes. Actually, it goes great even as a cold leftover out of a tupperware container sneakily eaten at 2AM.

Serves: 4. 8
Preparation Time: 10 minutes
Cooking Time: 5 minutes

INGREDIENTS:

Olive oil to taste
Salt and pepper to taste
(1 cup) Onion, quartered
(2 cups) Carrots, chunks
(2 cups) Turnips, quartered

(2 cups) Celery, chunks
(3 cups) Potatoes, quartered
(1 ½ cup) Water/chicken stock
(2 ½ lbs) Chicken breast, boneless, skinless, cubes

PREPARATION:

1. Place the chicken in a baking dish.

2. Coat the chicken evenly with salt and pepper to taste.

COOKING STEPS:

1. Hit BEANS/LENTILS and set time to default (5 minutes).

2. Heat the oil and brown the chicken thoroughly.

3. Add remaining ingredients and the water/broth.

4. Place lid on cooker, lock the PRESSURE SEAL, and bring up to pressure.

5. Once done, release pressure by quick release method.

6. Bring chicken to a platter and serve with the accumulated sauce, rice and salad.

Chicken Teriyaki

This is a great classic recipe now converted to your pressure cooker. The chicken thighs cook perfectly under a rich sauce, creating a unique caramel toned dish that goes very well with rice and salad. You can also perfect this by serving it with your favorite steamed vegetables. But watch out for the salt, as the soy sauce is already rich in sodium.

Serves: 4 - 6
Preparation Time: 20 minutes
Cooking Time: 20 minutes

INGREDIENTS:

Peanut oil to taste.

Salt and pepper to taste

(2 tbsp) Ginger, ground

(2 tbsp) Garlic, powder

(¼ cup) Brown sugar

(¾ cup) Soy sauce

(¼ cup) Apple cider vinegar

(1 cup) Chicken stock

(20 oz) Crushed pineapple

(3 lbs) Chicken thighs, boneless, skinless

COOKING STEPS:

1. Hit MEAT/CHICKEN followed by TIME ADJUSTMENT and correct time to 20 minutes.

2. Heat the oil and sauté the chicken for a couple of minute. Season to taste.

3. Add all the remaining ingredients. Stir to combine.

4. Place lid on cooker, lock the PRESSURE SEAL, and bring up to pressure.

5. Once done, release pressure by quick release method.

6. Bring chicken to a platter and serve with the accumulated sauce.

Coq au Vin

This is the chicken version of the Beef Bourguignon. It brings the same technique in a new taste, layering the bacon, the wine, and the chicken in a soup of heavens. Cooked for only 20 minutes, this light stew could warm up winter nights faster than an electric blanket. Enjoy it with loved ones for a fully satisfying meal.

Serves: 4
Preparation Time: 5 minutes
Cooking Time: 20 minutes

INGREDIENTS:

Salt and pepper to taste
Olive oil to taste
Flour, corn, wheat, to thicken
(1 tbsp) Thyme, dry
(1 tbsp) Bay leaves
(1 tbsp) Garlic, minced
(1 cup) Onion, chopped
(2 tbsp) Red wine vinegar

(1 cup) Parsley, chopped
(1 cup) Red dry wine
(1 cup) Tomato sauce
(1 cup) Chicken stock
(2 cups) Mushroom, sliced
(2 cups) Carrots, diced
(4 oz) Bacon, diced
(3 lbs) Chicken thighs, boneless, skinless

COOKING STEPS:

1. Hit SOUP/STEW followed by TIME ADJUSTMENT and correct time to 20 minutes.

2. Add the bacon and sauté until brown. No oil is necessary.

3. Add chicken, onions, garlic, herbs and mushrooms. Sauté until the onions are soft and mushrooms are brown. Season to taste.

4. Pour in the stock, the wine and the tomato sauce. Stir to combine.

4. Place lid on cooker, lock the PRESSURE SEAL, and bring up to pressure.

5. Once done, release pressure by quick release method.

6. Stir to combine. Bring dish to bowls and serve with a top of fresh parsley.

Creamy Chicken and Broccoli

If there's cheese and chicken, it must be good. This dish mixes the simplicity of the broccoli with the rich taste of dried spices to make your chicken win against fast food. And it's almost as fast as the pizza delivery guy: 20 minutes. Oh, did we mention there's cheese?

Serves: 4 - 6
Preparation Time: 15 minutes
Cooking Time: 5 minutes

INGREDIENTS:

Salt, black and red pepper to taste
Olive oil to taste
(1 tbsp) Dried parsley
(½ cup) Onion, chopped
(1 cup) Mozzarella cheese, shredded

(1 cup) Chicken broth
(4 cups) Broccoli, chopped
(4 oz) Cream cheese, cubes
(2 lb) Chicken breasts, boneless, skinless, chunks

PREPARATION:

1. Place the chicken in a baking dish.

2. Coat the chicken evenly with salt and pepper to taste.

COOKING STEPS:

1. Hit MEAT/CHICKEN followed by TIME ADJUSTMENT and correct time to 5 minutes.

2. Heat the oil and sauté the chicken for a couple of minute.

3. Add the remaining ingredients (besides the two cheeses), the chicken stock and give it a good stir to combine.

4. Place lid on cooker, lock the PRESSURE SEAL, and bring up to pressure.

5. Once done, release pressure by quick release method.

6. Add both cheeses to the pot and let it melt while stirring.

7. Place dish on platter and serve.

Lemongrass Coconut Chicken

This dish is a hidden gem from the East. The lightness of the coconut milk makes it a great replacement for cream. And the fresh lemongrass can be tasted even when used in small quantities. Even the chicken is happy to be served in such a sauce. Goes perfectly well with Jasmine rice or rice noodles.

Serves: 4
Preparation Time: 15 minutes
Cooking Time: 15 minutes

INGREDIENTS:

Olive Oil to taste
Salt and pepper to taste
(1 tbsp) Ginger, chopped
(3 tbsp) Coconut, ground
(4 tbsp) Garlic, crushed
(¼ cup) Cilantro, chopped

(1 ½ cup) Coconut milk
(½ cup) Lime, juiced
(1/2 cup) Lemongrass, chunks
(1 cup) Onion, sliced
(1 cup) Fish stock
(2 ½ lbs) Chicken legs, skinless

PREPARATION:

1. Combine lemongrass, garlic, ginger, fish sauce, coconut sugar, and the coconut milk into a blender or food processor. Reserve.

2. Salt and pepper the chicken to taste.

COOKING STEPS:

1. Hit MEAT/CHICKEN followed by TIME ADJUSTMENT and correct time to 15 minutes.

2. Heat the oil, sauté the chicken and the onion until brown.

3. Add the reserved sauce. Stir to combine.

4. Place lid on cooker, lock the PRESSURE SEAL, and bring up to pressure.

5. Once done, release pressure by quick release method.

6. Place dish on platter and serve.

Moroccan Chicken

It's time to experiment with spices. The cumin and the coriander will definitely steal the show, transforming the chicken and the squash into a delicious dark-red toned, very fragrant dish. It goes amazingly well with a simple Jasmine rice.

Serves: 4 - 6
Preparation Time: 10 minutes
Cooking Time: 15 minutes

INGREDIENTS:

Olive oil to taste
Salt and cayenne pepper to taste
(1 tbsp) Ginger, grated
(1 tbsp) Cumin, ground
(2 tbsp) Coriander, ground
(2 tbsp) Garlic, minced
(½ cup) Raisins, dry

(16 oz) Chickpeas, canned
(1 cup) Onions, sliced
(1 ½ cup) Water/chicken stock
(½ lb) Carrots, chunks
(2 lbs) Butternut squash, chunks
(3 lbs) Chicken breast, boneless, chunks

PREPARATION:

1. Place the chicken in a baking dish.
2. Coat the chicken evenly with salt and pepper to taste.

COOKING STEPS:

1. Hit MEAT/CHICKEN followed by TIME ADJUSTMENT and correct time to 15 minutes.

2. Heat the oil, sauté the chicken, the onion, the garlic and the spices until brown.

3. Add the squash, the carrots, the chickpeas and the water/stock. Give it a good stir.

4. Place lid on cooker, lock the PRESSURE SEAL, and bring up to pressure.

5. Once done, release pressure by quick release method.

6. Place dish on platter and serve.

One Pot Chicken Lentil Soup

This recipe has so much taste you don't even need to brown the ingredients beforehand. Just add everything at once and watch your pressure cooker do the miracle. Actually, don't watch it. Go do something better with your time. Just come back to the kitchen when it's time to eat. Serve it with big chunks of bread.

Serves: 4 - 6
Preparation Time: 5 minutes
Cooking Time: 30 minutes

INGREDIENTS:

Salt and pepper to taste
(1 tbsp) Cumin, ground
(1 tbsp) Oregano
(3 tbsp) Garlic, crushed
(½ cup) Tomatoes, diced

(½ cup) Cilantro, chopped
(2 cups) Onions, chopped
(7 cups) Water/chicken stock
(48 oz) Chicken thighs, skinless, boneless
(1 lb) Green lentils, dry

COOKING STEPS:

1. Add every ingredient in the pot.

2. Hit SOUP/STEW followed by TIME ADJUSTMENT and correct time to 30 minutes.

3. Place lid on cooker, lock the PRESSURE SEAL, and bring up to pressure.

4. Once done, release pressure by quick release method.

5. Stir it well. It can be served directly in the same pot.

Pesto Potato Chicken

Don't worry if you can't make your own pesto sauce. This recipe goes well with any ready-made option from your grocery store, just be thoughtful with the extra salt you add. The potatoes will cook until soft and the beautiful mixture of green and yellow flavors and colors will numb your senses for a few hours. Don't eat and drive!

Serves: 6 - 8
Preparation Time: 5 minutes
Cooking Time: 15 minutes

INGREDIENTS:

Olive oil to taste.
Salt and pepper to taste.
(⅓ cup) Pesto sauce
(1 ½ cup) Chicken stock

(1 cup) Onion, sliced
(1 lb) Potatoes, quartered
(1 lb) Carrots, small chunks
(3 lbs) Chicken thighs, skinless

PREPARATION:

1. Place the chicken in a baking dish.
2. Coat the chicken evenly with salt and pepper to taste.

COOKING STEPS:

1. Hit MEAT/CHICKEN followed by TIME ADJUSTMENT and correct time to 15 minutes.

2. Heat the oil, sauté the chicken and the onion until brown.

3. Add the pesto, the potatoes, the carrots and the chicken stock. Give it a good stir.

4. Place lid on cooker, lock the PRESSURE SEAL, and bring up to pressure.

5. Once done, release pressure by quick release method.

6. Place dish on platter and serve.

Black Beans, Rice and Chicken Chipotle

Now that's a real tasting fast food. In 20 minutes you can call the family and serve dinner. But be aware: the aromatic mixture of spices might also call on the neighbours. Good thing it serves up to 6 people. It goes deliciously well with grated cheese, guacamole and sour cream.

Serves: 6
Preparation Time: 5 minutes
Cooking Time: 20 minutes

INGREDIENTS:

Salt and pepper to taste
(1 tbsp) Chipotle peppers in adobo puree
(2 tbsp) Ghee or coconut oil
(4 tbsp) Lime, juiced
(1 cup) Rice, uncooked
(1 cup) Black beans (canned is fine) drained, rinsed

(1 cup) Onion, chopped
(1 ½ cup) Water/chicken stock
(3 cups) Tomatoes, diced
(2 lb) Chicken breast or thighs, boneless, skinless, chunks

PREPARATION:

1. Place the chicken in a baking dish.

2. Coat the chicken evenly with salt and pepper to taste.

COOKING STEPS:

1. Add every ingredient to the pot, besides the beans. Stir it well.

2. Hit MEAT/CHICKEN followed by TIME ADJUSTMENT and correct time to 20 minutes.

3. Place lid on cooker, lock the PRESSURE SEAL, and bring up to pressure.

4. Once done, release pressure by quick release method.

5. Add beans, stir to combine. Let remaining heat cook beans for a few minutes.

6. Place the dish in a platter and serve.

Lemon and Herbs Chicken

The acidity of the lemon breaks the chicken fat, making this dish both delicious and light. It's perfect for a family summer lunch or unplanned potlucks. Try to use fresh herbs instead of dry ones. Serve with rice or potatoes and be ready for the compliments.

Serves: 6
Preparation Time: 5 minutes
Cooking Time: 20 minutes

INGREDIENTS:

Salt and pepper to taste
Olive oil to taste.
(2 tbsp) Fresh oregano, chopped
(1 tbsp) Fresh basil, chopped
(4 tbsp) Garlic, chopped
(¼ cup) Lemon juice

(½ cup) Onion, chopped
(½ cup) Celery, chopped
(1 cup) Chicken broth
(1 cup) Fresh parsley, chopped
(1 cup) Black olives
(3 lbs) Chicken, whole, cut up

PREPARATION:

1. Place the chicken in a baking dish.

2. Coat the chicken evenly with salt and pepper to taste.

COOKING STEPS:

1. Hit MEAT/CHICKEN followed by TIME ADJUSTMENT and correct time to 20 minutes.

2. Heat the oil. Sauté the chicken, the herbs, the garlic and the onion until brown.

3. Add the lemon juice and the chicken stock. Bring the remaining ingredients (save the olives for serving) and stir it well.

4. Place lid on cooker, lock the PRESSURE SEAL, and bring up to pressure.

5. Once done, release pressure by quick release method.

6. Place dish on platter, add the olives and serve.

Chicken Adobo

This classic Filipino recipe is usually done over 2 hours. But good news: it will take only 45 minutes to do it under high-pressure. Remember to pour the delicious thick sauce over the meal. Watch out for the salt and the soy sauce, it has lots of sodium already. Make it perfect with rice and a selfie of a big happy and hungry family.

Serves: 6
Preparation Time: 5 minutes
Cooking Time: 45 minutes

INGREDIENTS:

Salt and pepper to taste
(1 tbsp) Garlic, crushed
(1 tbsp) Ginger, sliced
(2 tbsp) Bay leaves

(¼ cup) Vinegar
(1/2 cup) Soy sauce
(1 cup) Onion, chopped
(2 lbs) Chicken, whole, cut-up

COOKING STEPS:

1. Add every ingredient in the pot. Stir it well.

2. Hit MEAT/CHICKEN followed by TIME ADJUSTMENT and correct time to 45 minutes.

3. Place lid on cooker, lock the PRESSURE SEAL, and bring up to pressure.

4. Once done, release pressure by quick release method.

5. Stir it well, place on platter and serve.

Chicken Cacciatore

If cacciatore means hunter in Italian, this dish could be considered the Italian Hunter's Pot. The legendary boiling soup that the inns and caravans would cook for the travelers. Each new hunter would bring in his game, adding parts to the soup and eating from the pot. This boiling deliciousness used to be cooked for over days. Here we bring you a 35 minute version that loses none of the flavor or aroma. Behold the tomato, the chicken and the mushroom!

Serves: 6 to 8
Preparation Time: 5 minutes
Cooking Time: 30 minutes

INGREDIENTS:

Olive oil to taste
Salt, red and black pepper to taste
Parsley to taste
(2 tbsp) Tomato paste
(2 tbsp) Garlic, crushed
(1 cup) Green bell pepper, seeded & diced

(1 cup) Onions, chopped
(1 cup) Chicken/vegetable stock
(1 cup) Black olives
(10 oz) Mushrooms, sliced
(2 cups) Tomatoes, crushed
(3 lbs) Chicken breasts, boneless, skinless

PREPARATION:

1. Place the chicken in a baking dish.

2. Coat the chicken evenly with salt and pepper to taste.

COOKING STEPS:

1. Hit MEAT/CHICKEN followed by TIME ADJUSTMENT and correct time to 30 minutes.

2. Heat the oil. Sauté the chicken, the bell peppers, the mushroom, the garlic and the shallots until brown.

3. Add the crushed tomato, the paste and the stock. Stir to combine.

4. Place lid on cooker, lock the PRESSURE SEAL, and bring up to pressure.

5. Once done, release pressure by slow release method.

6. Add the olives, stir it well.

7. Place dish over platter, serve with fresh parsley.

Chicken Gumbo

That's what you get when you mix French and African cuisine. This classic Louisiana dish is the symbol of American diversification, uniting several cooking techniques from Europe and Africa in the big melting pot of the new continent. Hundreds of Gumbo varieties exist, but here, we come clean and simple with a light chicken version without seafood. Go for it and bon appetite!

Serves: 4 - 5
Preparation Time: 5 minutes
Cooking Time: 15 minutes

INGREDIENTS:

Salt and pepper to taste
Olive oil to taste
Flour (corn, wheat) to thicken
(2 tbsp) Thyme, dry
(2 tbsp)Paprika, dry
(2 tbsp) Garlic, chopped
(1 cup) Green bell pepper, diced

(1 cup) Onions, sliced
(1 cup) Celery, diced
(2 cups) Tomatoes, diced
(2 cups) Chicken stock
(1 lb) Chicken thighs, boneless, skinless
(1 lb) Smoked sausage

COOKING STEPS:

1. Hit MEAT/CHICKEN followed by TIME ADJUSTMENT and correct time to 15 minutes.

2. Heat the oil and sauté the chicken, the sausage the garlic, the onion, the celery and the bell peppers until brown. Season to taste.

3. Add the remaining ingredients and stir to combine.

4. Place lid on cooker, lock the PRESSURE SEAL, and bring up to pressure.

5. Once done, release pressure by slow release method, letting the steam escape naturally.

6. Bring dish to bowl and serve along rice.

Chicken Alfredo Pasta

Why buy the ready-made sauce when you can easily cook your own Alfredo pasta quickly under pressure? All you need is butter, pasta and parmesan to make the traditional Italian style. You can't err this. Add more cream and seasoning for the copycat of that ready-made Alfredo in a jar. In 7 minutes, you can call the family and the feast begins.

Serves: 4 - 5
Preparation Time: 5 minutes
Cooking Time: 7 minutes

INGREDIENTS:

Salt and pepper to taste
Butter to taste
(2 tbsp) Oregano, dry
(2 tbsp) Thyme, dry
(2 tbsp) Garlic, chopped
(½ cup) Cream

(1 cup) Onions, diced
(1 cup) Parsley, chopped
(1 cup) Parmesan, grated
(2 cups) Chicken stock
(8 oz) Pasta, dry
(1 lb) Chicken thighs, boneless, skinless, diced

COOKING STEPS:

1. Hit RICE/RISOTTO followed by TIME ADJUSTMENT and correct time to 7 minutes.

2. Heat the butter and sauté the chicken, the garlic and the onion until brown. Season to taste.

3. Add remaining ingredients (save the cheese and the parsley for serving) and stir to combine.

4. Place lid on cooker, lock the PRESSURE SEAL, and bring up to pressure.

5. Once done, release pressure by slow release method, letting the steam escape naturally.

6. Bring dish to bowl and top with cheese and parsley.

Honey Cashew Chicken

Born Chinese, this dish is now a great example of the international cosmopolitan cuisine of the modern fast food Asian restaurant. The honey caramelizes the chicken as the cashew brings that crispy and crunchy taste to seal this dish in style. Serve it with rice and vegetables for a home-made variation of the classic take-away meal.

Serves: 4
Preparation Time: 5 minutes
Cooking Time: 5 minutes

INGREDIENTS:

Salt and pepper to taste
Peanut oil to taste
(2 tbsp) Garlic, chopped
(3 tbsp) Honey
(½ cup) Chicken stock
(1 cup) Onions, diced

(1 cup) Red bell pepper, diced
(1 cup) Cashews, roasted, unsalted
(2 cups) Broccoli
(1 lb) Chicken breast, boneless, skinless, diced

COOKING STEPS:

1. Hit MEAT/CHICKEN followed by TIME ADJUSTMENT and correct time to 5 minutes.

2. Heat the oil and sauté the chicken, the garlic and the onion until brown. Season to taste.

3. Add remaining ingredients and stir to combine.

4. Place lid on cooker, lock the PRESSURE SEAL, and bring up to pressure.

5. Once done, release pressure by slow release method, letting the steam escape naturally.

6. Bring dish to bowl and serve along rice and steamed vegetables.

Honey Mustard Chicken

This classic roast recipe makes a cameo in this book with a radical transformation. Now the chicken caramelizes with the honey and the mustard absorbs the vegetables in a delicious thick sauce. This is a great example of a converted recipe, demonstrating how easily you can adapt any ingredient for pressure-cooking.

Serves: 4 - 5
Preparation Time: 5 minutes
Cooking Time: 10 minutes

INGREDIENTS:

Salt and pepper to taste
Vegetable oil to taste
(2 tbsp) Rosemary, dry
(2 tbsp) Garlic, chopped
(½ cup) Honey

(½ cup) Mustard, dijon is great
(1 cup) Onions, chopped
(1 cup) Vegetable stock
(2 cups) Carrots, sliced
(1 lb) Chicken breast, diced

COOKING STEPS:

1. Hit BEANS/LENTILS followed by TIME ADJUSTMENT and correct time to 10 minutes.

2. Heat the oil and sauté the onion, the garlic and the chicken until brown. Season to taste.

3. Add remaining ingredients gradually and stir to combine. Season to taste.

4. Place lid on cooker, lock the PRESSURE SEAL, and bring up to pressure.

5. Once done, release pressure by quick release method.

6. Bring dish to plates and serve along rice, salad or steamed vegetables.

Peach Whisky Chicken

Truth be told, the fashion of whisky in food is an invention of the marketing industry. And it worked amazingly well. The strong aroma can be compared to brandy and wine based dishes. The peach balances the sweet and savory tastes brilliantly. The barbecue sauce adds that thick and rich consistency. And in 10 minutes you can already smell the delicious dinner coming along. Serve it with mashed potatoes, vegetables and pour in the sauce for an envious gravy.

Serves: 4
Preparation Time: 5 minutes
Cooking Time: 10 minutes

INGREDIENTS:

Salt and pepper to taste
Olive oil to taste
(2 tbsp) Garlic, chopped
(½ cup) Chicken stock
(½ cup) BBQ sauce

(1 cup) Onions, diced
(1 cup) Whisky, malt or bourbon
(2 cups) Peaches, pitted, diced
(1 lb) Chicken breast, boneless, skinless, diced

COOKING STEPS:

1. Hit MEAT/CHICKEN followed by TIME ADJUSTMENT and correct time to 10 minutes.

2. Heat the oil and sauté the chicken, the garlic and the onion until brown. Season to taste.

3. Add remaining ingredients and stir to combine.

4. Place lid on cooker, lock the PRESSURE SEAL, and bring up to pressure.

5. Once done, release pressure by slow release method, letting the steam escape naturally.

6. Bring dish to bowl and serve along mashed potatoes and steamed vegetables.

Indian Butter Chicken

Butter and curry, hm, this lovely emulsion of tastes is one of the bases of Indian cuisine. Substitute butter for ghee and, wow, sparks will fly. There are hundreds of ready-made spices out there in case you want a blend of all those tastes in one place. Just make sure you have the turmeric and the cumin. And the curry, of course!

Serves: 4 - 5
Preparation Time: 5 minutes
Cooking Time: 10 minutes

INGREDIENTS:

Butter to taste
Salt and pepper to taste
(1 tbsp) Cumin, ground
(1 tbsp) Curry, ground
(1 ½ tbsp) Paprika, ground
(2 tbsp) Garlic, chopped
(2 tbsp) Ginger, ground
(2 tbsp) Turmeric, ground
(½ cup) Cilantro, chopped
(1 cup) Onions, diced
(1 cup) Carrots, diced
(1 cup) Tomatoes, diced
(1 cup) Vegetable stock
(2 cups) Coconut milk
(2 lbs) Chicken thighs, skinless, boneless, diced

COOKING STEPS:

1. Hit MEAT/CHICKEN followed by TIME ADJUSTMENT and correct time to 10 minutes.

2. Melt the butter and brown the chicken, the onions and the garlic until brown. Season to taste.

3. Add carrots, tomato, the stock and spices. Stir to combine.

4. Place lid on cooker, lock the PRESSURE SEAL, and bring up to pressure.

5. Once done, release pressure by quick release method.

6. Add the coconut milk and the cilantro. Stir to combine. Transfer to bowls and serve with rice and salad.

Vietnamese Pho

This is a delicious white soup served with noodles. After 40 minutes the chicken should almost dissolve under the fluids, creating a combination of tastes that will make your mouth travel to a Vietnamese hut by the beach. Add a dash of lemon is for an optional but delicious serving treat.

Serves: 4 - 5
Preparation Time: 10 minutes (plus 10 minutes for cooking the noodles)
Cooking Time: 40 minutes

INGREDIENTS:

Vegetable oil to taste
Salt and pepper to taste
(1 tbsp) Ginger, ground
(1 tbsp) Coriander, ground
(2 tbsp) Garlic, chopped
(1 cup) Onions, diced

(1 cup) Cilantro, chopped
(4 cups) Fish stock
(3 cups) Pho noodles, cooked
(2 lbs) Chicken breast, boneless, skinless, chunks

COOKING STEPS:

1. Add every ingredient to the pot (save the noodles and the cilantro for serving)

 and season to taste. Stir to combine.

2. Hit MEAT/CHICKEN followed by TIME ADJUSTMENT and correct time to 40 minutes.

3. Place lid on cooker, lock the PRESSURE SEAL, and bring up to pressure.

4. Once done, release pressure by slow release method, letting the steam escape naturally.

5. Bring dish to bowl. Serve with Pho noodles and cilantro.

Balsamic Onion Chicken

Balsamic vinegar is one of the simplest but richest tastes of the Italian cuisine. The dark tone sauce makes it great pair with a simple white rice or mashed potato. And the caramelized onions blend with the chicken perfectly - as always. Done in super fast 20 minutes, it will take you longer to set the table.

Serves: 4 - 5
Preparation Time: 10 minutes
Cooking Time: 20 minutes

INGREDIENTS:

Vegetable oil to taste
Salt and pepper to taste
(2 tbsp) Garlic, chopped
(2 cups) Onions, chopped

(1 cup) Balsamic vinegar
(1 cup) Vegetable stock
(2 lbs) Chicken breast, boneless, skinless, chunks

COOKING STEPS:

1. Hit MEAT/CHICKEN followed by TIME ADJUSTMENT and correct time to 20 minutes.

2. Heat the oil and sauté the chicken, the garlic and the onions until brown. Season to taste.

3. Add the stock and the vinegar. Stir to combine.

4. Place lid on cooker, lock the PRESSURE SEAL, and bring up to pressure.

5. Once done, release pressure by quick release method.

6. Bring dish to bowl. Serve with mashed potatoes and steamed vegetables.

Buffalo Wings

The ultimate party food done in half the time. By starting the cooking process in the pressure cooker, you make sure the chicken gets soft and well done. But at the end we ask you to cheat a little bit and use the oven. In a total of 20 minutes, you get the best of the two worlds: the juiciness of the pressure cooker and the crispness of the oven.

Serves: 4 - 5
Preparation Time: 5 minutes
Cooking Time: 10 minutes (plus 10 minutes in the oven)

INGREDIENTS:

Vegetable oil to taste
Salt and pepper to taste
(½ cup) Honey

(½ cup) Tomato paste/puree
(2 cups) Water
(2 lbs) Chicken wings

COOKING STEPS:

1. Add STEAM TRAY to the pot and drop in water. Place the chicken over the tray and make sure they are not covered in water. Season to taste.

2. Hit MEAT/CHICKEN followed by TIME ADJUSTMENT and correct time to 10 minutes.

3. Place lid on cooker, lock the PRESSURE SEAL, and bring up to pressure.

4. Once done, release pressure by quick release method.

5. In a mixing bowl, add the honey, the tomato paste and the chicken wings. Season to taste and toss to combine until chicken is coated in sauce.

6. Bring chicken to a baking bowl and roast it for 10 minutes in the oven before serving.

PORK

Caldo Verde

This is Portuguese for "green broth", but you can call it kale soup. This dish is a classic European relic, usually cooked for hours over the stove. But here, under high-pressure, this boiling tasting miracle needs only 20 minutes to surprise you. The smoked sausage is a must, so don't be afraid of adding a bit more to the recipe.

Serves: 4 - 5
Preparation Time: 5 minutes
Cooking Time: 20 minutes

INGREDIENTS:

Salt and pepper to taste
(1 tbsp) Garlic
(2 tbsp) Thyme
(1 cup) Onion
(1 cup) Tomatoes, diced

(4 cups) Kale, chopped
(4 cups) Water/vegetable stock
(½ lb) Smoked sausage, sliced
(1 lbs) Potatoes, chunks

COOKING STEPS:

1. Hit CANNING/PRESERVING followed by TIME ADJUSTMENT and correct time to 20 minutes.

2. Add sausage to pot and sauté until brown. No fat is necessary. Add kale and stir to combine. Once the kale gets soft, remove all ingredient to a bowl and reserve.

3. Over the sausage fat, add the onion, the garlic, the herbs, the tomatoes, the water/stock and the potatoes. Stir to combine.

4. Place lid on cooker, lock the PRESSURE SEAL, and bring up to pressure.

5. Once done, release pressure by quick release method.

6. Bring the sausage and kale back into the pot and stir to combine. Bring to bowls and serve with chunks of bread.

Vindaloo

The Portuguese colonized the South India and that's all we got. A delicious ensemble of east and west techniques, the combinations of many colors, tastes and aromas. It's the footprint of our culinary history and now your family can have it for lunch. Enjoy it with rice and fresh salad.

Serves: 4 - 5
Preparation Time: 10 minutes
Cooking Time: 30 minutes

INGREDIENTS:

Salt and pepper to taste
Olive oil to taste
(1 tbsp) Paprika, ground
(1 tbsp) Cumin, ground
(1 tbsp) Mustard seeds
(2 tbsp) Red wine vinegar

(4 tbsp) Garlic, minced
(½ cup) Cilantro, chopped
(1 cup) Chicken broth
(1 cup) Tomatoes, diced
(2 cups) Onions, chopped
(3 lbs) Pork roast, trimmed

COOKING STEPS:

1. Hit CANNING/PRESERVING followed by TIME ADJUSTMENT and correct time to 30 minutes.

2. Heat the oil, add the onions the garlic and the pork. Season to taste. Sauté until every side of the meat is brown.

3. Add remaining ingredients. Stir to combine.

4. Place lid on cooker, lock the PRESSURE SEAL, and bring up to pressure.

5. Once done, release pressure by slow release method, letting the steam escape naturally.

6. Stir to combine. Bring to bowls and serve.

Feijoada

A classic Brazilian dish, this is a historical slave meal that mixes the leftover pork parts with black beans. Here we save you from pig tongues, ears and feet, replacing them for noble meat cuts and making the dish a bit lighter for first time eaters. Serve it with rice and kale for a delicious combination of flavors.

Serves: 4 - 5
Preparation Time: 10 minutes
Cooking Time: 40 minutes

INGREDIENTS:

Salt and pepper to taste
Vegetable oil to taste
(4 tbsp) Garlic, minced
(2 tbsp) Bay leaves
(2 cups) Onions, chopped
(½ lb) Pork belly, chunks

(½ lb) Pork ribs, chunks
(4 cups) Black beans, dry, soaked overnight
(4 cups) Water/ vegetable broth
(1 lb) Smoked pork sausage, sliced
(1 lb) Pork tenderloin, chunks

COOKING STEPS:

1. Hit CANNING/PRESERVING followed by TIME ADJUSTMENT and correct time to 30 minutes.

2. Heat the oil, add the onions the garlic and the pork. Season to taste. Sauté until every side of the meat is brown.

3. Add remaining ingredients. Stir to combine.

4. Place lid on cooker, lock the PRESSURE SEAL, and bring up to pressure.

5. Once done, release pressure by slow release method, letting the steam escape naturally.

6. Stir to combine. Bring to plates and serve along stir-fried kale, rice and hot pepper sauce.

Afelia

This Greek dish stirs pork, mushrooms and red wine into an ambrosia of tastes. The coriander adds the aroma that makes it unique. And the potatoes render the dish rich and correct. It's a family holiday trip that can be appreciated from your dinner table.

Serves: 4 - 5
Preparation Time: 10 minutes
Cooking Time: 40 minutes

INGREDIENTS:

Salt and pepper to taste
Vegetable oil to taste
(1 tbsp) Coriander, dry
(4 tbsp) Garlic, minced
(1 cup) Dry red wine

(2 cups) Onions, chopped
(2 cups) Mushrooms, sliced
(3 cups) Water/vegetable broth
(4 cups) Potatoes, chunks
(1 lb) Pork tenderloin, chunks

COOKING STEPS:

1. Hit CANNING/PRESERVING followed by TIME ADJUSTMENT and correct time to 30 minutes.

2. Heat the oil, add the onions the garlic and the pork. Season to taste. Sauté until every side of the meat is brown.

3. Add remaining ingredients. Stir to combine.

4. Place lid on cooker, lock the PRESSURE SEAL, and bring up to pressure.

5. Once done, release pressure by slow release method, letting the steam escape naturally.

6. Stir to combine. Bring to bowls and serve it with a spoonful of yogurt.

Goulash

This famous European dish was unmercifully stolen and rebranded throughout the whole continent. But we know its humble origins in Hungary and keep it classic here. The pork, the paprika and the wine trio is ever present to bring the aroma that made this dish so desirable by kings and peasants. Feast it with potatoes for a full meal.

Serves: 4 - 5
Preparation Time: 10 minutes
Cooking Time: 30 minutes

INGREDIENTS:

Salt and pepper to taste
Vegetable oil to taste
(1 tbsp) Oregano, dry
(2 tbsp) Paprika, dry
(1 cup) Dry red wine

(2 cups) Tomatoes, diced
(2 cups) Onions, chopped
(2 cups) Vegetable broth
(1 ½ lb) Pork shoulder, boneless, chunks

COOKING STEPS:

1. Hit CANNING/PRESERVING followed by TIME ADJUSTMENT and correct time to 30 minutes.

2. Heat the oil, add the onions and the pork. Season to taste. Sauté until every side of the meat is brown.

3. Add remaining ingredients. Stir to combine.

4. Place lid on cooker, lock the PRESSURE SEAL, and bring up to pressure.

5. Once done, release pressure by slow release method, letting the steam escape naturally.

6. Stir to combine. Bring to plates and serve along mashed potatoes.

Egg Roll Soup

The delicious taste of egg rolls, now in a soup. We took the fabulous inside of the classic Asian entreé, and transform it into a blasting tasting pork soup. Under pressure, the meat dissolves itself into a intense sauce. The cabbage brings in a light color, a fresh taste to the dish. Serve it along with soy sauce, rice noodles or Jasmine rice and salad.

Serves: 8.10
Preparation Time: 10 minutes
Cooking Time: 25 minutes

INGREDIENTS:

Vegetable oil to taste

Salt and pepper to taste

(1 tbsp) Ginger, ground

(1 cup) Onions, diced

(2 cups) 1/2 head cabbage, chopped

(2 cups) Carrots, shredded

(4 cups) Vegetable broth

(1 lb) Pork, ground

COOKING STEPS:

1. Hit MEAT/CHICKEN followed by TIME ADJUSTMENT and correct time to 25 minutes.
3. Heat the oil. Sauté the pork and the onion until brown. Season as desired.
4. Add the cabbage, the carrots and the broth. Adjust with salt if necessary. Stir it well.
5. Place lid on cooker, lock the PRESSURE SEAL, and bring up to pressure.
6. Once done, release pressure by quick release method.
7. Give it a good stir. It can be served directly in the pot.

One-Pot Pork Chops

A one pot miracle for you to save the day. This recipe tenders the chops brilliantly. And the potatoes add that rich and delicious starchy taste. You can thicken the sauce by adding a spoon or two of flour (wheat, barley, manioc) or by letting it cook slowly over time. It's so rich and tasty, the only thing missing for a full meal is a spoon.

Serves: 4 - 6
Preparation Time: 10 minutes
Cooking Time: 35 minutes

INGREDIENTS:

Salt and pepper to taste
Butter to taste
(3 tbsp) Worcestershire sauce
(1 cup) Carrots, chunks

(1 cup) Onions, chopped
(1 cup) Vegetable broth
(1 ½ lb) Potatoes, chunks
(2 ½ lbs) Pork chops

PREPARATION:

1. Place the pork in a baking dish.

2. Coat the pork evenly with salt and pepper to taste.

COOKING STEPS:

1. Hit MEAT/CHICKEN followed by TIME ADJUSTMENT and correct time to 35 minutes.

2. Heat the butter. Sauté the pork chops and the onion until brown.

3. Add the Worcestershire sauce, the carrots, the broth and the potatoes.

4. Place lid on cooker, lock the PRESSURE SEAL, and bring up to pressure.

5. Once done, release pressure by quick release method.

6. Give it a good stir. It can be served directly in the pot.

Kalua Pig

One of the most famous dishes from Hawaii is this pig cooked in an oven buried under the soil. It tastes deliciously but with a price: it takes 6 hours to be prepared. But now under pressure, just 90 minutes gets it done. Be ready to be giving the leftovers and the recipe away.

Serves: 8
Preparation Time: 10 minutes
Cooking Time: 90 minutes

INGREDIENTS:

Salt and pepper to taste
(6 tbsp) Garlic, whole
(1 ½ cup) Water/ vegetable stock

(3 cups) Cabbage, wedges
(½ lb) Bacon, slices
(5 lbs) Pork shoulder roast, big chunks

PREPARATION:

1. Place the pork in a baking dish.

2. Coat the pork evenly with salt and pepper to taste.

COOKING STEPS:

1. Hit MEAT/CHICKEN followed by TIME ADJUSTMENT and correct time to 90 minutes.

2. Sauté the bacon until brown and

3. Add the pork roast over the bacon. Pour in the water/stock.

4. Place lid on cooker, lock the PRESSURE SEAL, and bring up to pressure.

5. Once done, release pressure by quick release method.

6. Remove pork shoulder to a bowl and shred it with a fork.

7. Add shredded pork and cabbage to pot. Hit FISH/VEGETABLE/STEAM followed by TIME ADJUSTMENT and correct time to 4 minutes.

8. Place lid on cooker, lock the PRESSURE SEAL, and bring up to pressure.

9. Once done, release pressure by quick release method.

10. Give it a good stir to combine. Serve each plate individually with a generous portion of the pork roast and the cabbage on the side.

Pulled Pork Carnitas

Pork shoulders are already very tender by nature. Now imagine it done in shreds and under high-pressure. This classic Mexican recipes gains a new twist and a very new cooking time: only 1 hour for what would usually take 2, at least! It sits perfectly next to tortillas, wraps and salads, serving sunday lunches and potlucks.

Serves: 6 to 8
Preparation Time: 20 minutes
Cooking Time: 60 minutes

INGREDIENTS:

Canola oil to taste
Salt and pepper to taste
(1 tbsp) Poblano peppers, chopped
(2 tbsp) Garlic, chopped
(2 tbsp) Coriander, chopped
(3 tbsp) Cumin, ground

(1 tbsp) Jalapeno peppers, chopped
(1 tbsp) Serrano pepper, chopped
(2 cups) Onions, chopped
(1 ½ cup) Beef broth
(3 lbs) Boneless pork shoulder, chunks

PREPARATION:

1. Place the pork in a baking dish.

2. Coat the pork evenly with salt and pepper to taste.

COOKING STEPS:

1. Hit MEAT/CHICKEN.

2. Heat the oil, sauté the pork shoulders until brown. Hit CANCEL.

3. Remove the pork and shred it with a fork.

4. Hit MEAT/CHICKEN again. Adjust time to 60 minutes.

5. Bring the pork shoulder back to the pot. Add the peppers, the onion, the garlic and the spices. Fill it up with the broth and give it a good stir to combine.

5. Place lid on cooker, lock the PRESSURE SEAL, and bring up to pressure.

6. Once done, release pressure by quick release method.

7. Stir it up and serve with guacamole, tomato salsa and wraps and salad.

Chickpea Sausage Soup

This Spanish style soup is a wonder of nature. The sausage almost dissolves itself in between the chickpeas. And the endives add that final touch that calls for a bigger bowl. But be aware when cooking chickpeas. They usually need only 1 hour under pressure to become soft and tasty, but they are famously unpredictable. Soak them in water overnight and be on the safe side.

Serves: 5 - 6
Preparation Time: 5 minutes
Cooking Time: 60 minutes

INGREDIENTS:

Salt and pepper to taste
Olive oil to taste
(2 tbsp) Garlic, chopped
(1 cup) Onions, chopped

(1 ½ cup) Chickpeas, dry, soaked overnight
(3 cups) Chicken stock
(4 cups) Endives, chopped
(1 lb) Smoked sausage, sliced

COOKING STEPS:

1. Hit BEANS/LENTILS followed by TIME ADJUSTMENT and correct time to 60 minutes.

2. Heat the oil and sauté the sausage, the garlic and the onion until brown. Season to taste.

3. Add remaining ingredients and stir to combine.

4. Place lid on cooker, lock the PRESSURE SEAL, and bring up to pressure.

5. Once done, release pressure by slow release method, letting the steam escape naturally.

6. Add endives and stir to combine. Bring dish to bowl and serve.

Pozole

The food from the Aztec gods. The Mexican party dish. The Pozole is such a simple soup that uniquely joins complex tastes and aromas. The hominy and the pork will dissolve under the boiling stew, expanding the sensibility of everyone at the table. And the avocado pops in at the end, freshening up the dish with a clean and nourishing touch.

Serves: 5 - 6
Preparation Time: 5 minutes
Cooking Time: 60 minutes

Ingredients:

Salt and pepper to taste
Olive oil to taste
(2 tbsp) Garlic, chopped
(1 cup) Onions, chopped

(2 cups) Chicken stock
(2 cups) Avocado, diced
(4 cups) Hominy, drained, rinsed
(1 ½ lb) Pork shoulder, chunks

Cooking Steps:

1. Hit BEANS/LENTILS followed by TIME ADJUSTMENT and correct time to 60 minutes.

2. Heat the oil and sauté the pork, the garlic and the onion until brown. Season to taste.

3. Add remaining ingredients (save the avocado for serving) and stir to combine.

4. Place lid on cooker, lock the PRESSURE SEAL, and bring up to pressure.

5. Once done, release pressure by slow release method, letting the steam escape naturally.

6. Bring dish to bowl, top with avocado and serve.

High-Pressure Pork Rice

This is the adaptation of the classic Chinese fried rice recipe for high-pressure cookers. And it works perfectly well. The pork roast doesn't need much time under intense stir to be done and in 5 minutes under high-pressure, the rice blends in flawlessly. Season in layers to find the perfect amount of salt.

Serves: 5 - 6
Preparation Time: 5 minutes
Cooking Time: 5 minutes

INGREDIENTS:

Salt and pepper to taste
Vegetable oil to taste
(2 tbsp) Garlic, chopped
(1 cup) Onions, chopped

(2 cups) Carrots, sliced
(3 cups) Vegetable stock
(2 cups) Rice, basmati works great
(1 lb) Pork roast, sliced

COOKING STEPS:

1. Hit BEANS/LENTILS followed by TIME ADJUSTMENT and correct time to 5 minutes.

2. Heat the oil and sauté the onion, the garlic and the pork until brown. Season to taste.

3. Add the carrots, the stock, the rice and stir to combine. Season to taste.

4. Place lid on cooker, lock the PRESSURE SEAL, and bring up to pressure.

5. Once done, release pressure by quick release method.

6. Bring dish to plates and serve along salad or steamed vegetables.

Cochinita Pibil

This is a memorable Mexican roasted meal, here adapted for your pressure cooker. What makes it stand out in the eyes are the banana leaves. You can find them in specialized supermarkets. Just follow the recipe and bring the dish to a bowl covered in banana leaves for a beautiful looking meal. And tasty!

Serves: 5 - 6
Preparation Time: 5 minutes
Cooking Time: 40 minutes

INGREDIENTS:

Vegetable oil to taste
Salt and pepper to taste
(1 ½ tbsp) Cumin
(1 ½ tbsp) Oregano
(2 tbsp) Garlic, chopped
(½ cup) Orange, juiced

(½ cup) White wine vinegar
(1 cup) Onions, diced
(1 cup) Tomatoes, diced
(1 cup) Vegetable stock
(1 cup) White wine, dry
(3 lbs) Pork shoulder roast, chunks

COOKING STEPS:

1. Add every ingredient to the pot and season to taste. Stir to combine.

2. Hit MEAT/CHICKEN followed by TIME ADJUSTMENT and correct time to 40 minutes.

3. Place lid on cooker, lock the PRESSURE SEAL, and bring up to pressure.

4. Once done, release pressure by slow release method, letting the steam escape naturally.

5. Bring dish to bowl. Serve with rice and black beans.

Pork, Prosciutto and Apple

This dish usually asks for a nice oven-made crispy tone. But here we converted what was a roast recipe into a brilliant braised pork with the same technique from the Beef Bourguignon and the Coq au Vin. Now the pork, the apple and the sage join together in a sauce that will surprise even the most skeptics. What a great mixture.

Serves: 4 - 5
Preparation Time: 10 minutes
Cooking Time: 30 minutes

INGREDIENTS:

Vegetable oil to taste
Salt and pepper to taste
(2 tbsp) Sage, whole
(1 cup) White wine, dry
(1 cup) Vegetable stock

(1 cup) Cheese (parmesan works great), grated
(2 cups) Apple, cored, diced
(12 oz) Ham (prosciutto or pancetta are great), slices
(2 lbs) Pork roast, chunks

COOKING STEPS:

1. Hit MEAT/CHICKEN followed by TIME ADJUSTMENT and correct time to 30 minutes.

2. Heat the oil, sauté the sage and the ham until brown. Reserve.

3. Add the pork roast and sauté until brown. Season to taste.

4. Add the apples, the stock, the wine, the sage, and the ham. Stir to combine.

3. Place lid on cooker, lock the PRESSURE SEAL, and bring up to pressure.

4. Once done, release pressure by slow release method, letting the steam escape naturally.

5. Bring dish to bowl. Top with cheese and serve.

BEEF

Stroganoff

This exceptional Russian dish is known for centuries. The wonders of mustard and beef gained the world and now you can even microwave it from a frozen package. But don't do it! Keep on reading and learn how to prepare this prodigy meal under high-pressure for only 20 minutes. It's worth every bite.

Serves: 4 - 5
Preparation Time: 10 minutes
Cooking Time: 20 minutes

INGREDIENTS:

Salt and pepper to taste
Vegetable oil to taste
(1 tbsp) Oregano, dry
(1 tbsp) Mustard
(1 tbsp) Flour, wheat
(1 cup) Dry white wine

(2 cups) Tomatoes, diced
(1 cup) Onions, chopped
(2 cups) Carrots, chunks
(1 cup) Meat broth
(1 lb) Mushrooms, sliced
(1 ½ lb) Lean beef, chunks

COOKING STEPS:

1. Hit CANNING/PRESERVING followed by TIME ADJUSTMENT and correct time to 20 minutes.

2. Heat the oil, add the onions and the pork. Season to taste. Sauté until every side of the meat is brown.

3. Add remaining ingredients. Stir to combine.

4. Place lid on cooker, lock the PRESSURE SEAL, and bring up to pressure.

5. Once done, release pressure by slow release method, letting the steam escape naturally.

6. Stir to combine. Bring to plates and serve along noodles or rice.

Oxtail Stew

This bone and gelatin rich meat is perfect for stews. It merges nicely with the broth and the legumes, creating a meal that can easily gather families around the dinner table. It's a classic dish for pressure cookers and I bet your grandma cooked it at large. Just bring everything to the pot and wait. That's the most important ingredient for stews: time.

Serves: 4 - 5
Preparation Time: 10 minutes
Cooking Time: 40 minutes

INGREDIENTS:

Salt and pepper to taste
Vegetable oil to taste
(1 tbsp) Thyme, dry
(1 tbsp) Rosemary, dry
(2 tbsp) Bay leaves
(1 cup) Dry red wine

(1 cup) Beef broth
(2 cups) Tomatoes, diced
(2 cups) Onions, chopped
(2 cups) Carrots, chunks
(2 lbs) Oxtail, chunks

COOKING STEPS:

1. Hit CANNING/PRESERVING followed by TIME ADJUSTMENT and correct time to 40 minutes.

2. Heat the oil, add the onions and the oxtail. Season to taste. Sauté until every side of the meat is brown.

3. Add remaining ingredients. Stir to combine.

4. Place lid on cooker, lock the PRESSURE SEAL, and bring up to pressure.

5. Once done, release pressure by slow release method, letting the steam escape naturally.

6. Stir to combine. Bring to bowls and serve along noodles or rice.

Beef and Ale Stew

Beef and beer. It's no wonder they sound similar. The fibers of the meat dissolve into a melting pot of tastes. Meanwhile, the dark stout beer boils even the hardest of the ingredients into tender bites of flavor. Hmm, is it dinner time already? Serve it with pasta, rice or big chunks of bread, so everyone can scoop up the delicious leftovers from the bottom of the bowl.

Serves: 4 - 5
Preparation Time: 10 minutes
Cooking Time: 30 minutes

INGREDIENTS:

Salt and pepper to taste
Vegetable oil to taste
(1 tbsp) Thyme, dry
(1 tbsp) Rosemary, dry
(2 tbsp) Bay leaves
(2 tbsp) Garlic, chopped

(1 cup) Beef broth
(2 cups) Onions, chopped
(2 cups) Carrots, chunks
(14 ½ oz) 1 can stout dark beer, Guinness works great
(2 ½ lbs) Beef stew meat, chunks

COOKING STEPS:

1. Hit CANNING/PRESERVING followed by TIME ADJUSTMENT and correct time to 30 minutes.

2. Heat the oil, add the onions, the garlic and the beef. Season to taste. Sauté until every side of the meat is brown.

3. Add remaining ingredients. Stir to combine.

4. Place lid on cooker, lock the PRESSURE SEAL, and bring up to pressure.

5. Once done, release pressure by slow release method, letting the steam escape naturally.

6. Stir to combine. Bring to bowls and serve along noodles or rice.

Chili con Carne

The official ambassador of Mexico all around the world, this dish needs no introductions. It's the perfect gathering meal, bringing together friends and family around tacos and wraps. Go easy on the hot peppers and let each one choose its own dose of spiciness.

Serves: 4 - 5
Preparation Time: 10 minutes
Cooking Time: 20 minutes

INGREDIENTS:

Salt and pepper to taste
Vegetable oil to taste
(1 tbsp) Cumin
(2 tbsp) Chilli peppers, seeded, chopped
(2 tbsp) Garlic, chopped
(1 tbsp) Apple cider vinegar

(½ cup) Cilantro, chopped
(2 cups) Tomatoes, chopped
(2 cups) Onions, chopped
(3 cups) Vegetable broth
(15 oz) Canned kidney beans, drained
(3 lbs) Beef chuck, ground

COOKING STEPS:

1. Hit CANNING/PRESERVING followed by TIME ADJUSTMENT and correct time to 20 minutes.

2. Heat the oil, add the onions, the garlic, the herbs and the beef. Season to taste. Sauté until brown.

3. Add remaining ingredients. Stir to combine.

4. Place lid on cooker, lock the PRESSURE SEAL, and bring up to pressure.

5. Once done, release pressure by quick release method.

6. Stir to combine. Bring to bowls and serve along tacos, wraps, salad, guacamole, sour cream, tomato salsa and hot sauce.

Beef Bourguignon

This classic French dish starts by sautéing beef roast over sizzling bacon. How could it go any wrong from then on? It's one of the most rich tasting stews ever, placing French cuisine up there in the rankings for the best food in the world. But enough talking, it's time to go to the butcher!

Serves: 4 - 5
Preparation Time: 10 minutes
Cooking Time: 20 minutes

INGREDIENTS:

Salt and pepper to taste
Olive oil to taste
(1 tbsp) Thyme, dry
(1 tbsp) Marjoram, dry
(2 tbsp) Garlic, chopped
(½ cup) Bacon, diced

(1 cup) Dry red wine
(2 cups) Mushrooms, sliced
(2 cups) Onions, chopped
(2 cups) Carrots, chopped
(2 cups) Beef broth
(2 lbs) Beef roast, chunks

COOKING STEPS:

1. Hit CANNING/PRESERVING followed by TIME ADJUSTMENT and correct time to 20 minutes.

2. Heat the pan and fry the bacon. No oil is necessary. Once brown, add the onions, the garlic and the beef. Season to taste. Sauté until every side of the meat is brown.

3. Add remaining ingredients. Stir to combine.

4. Place lid on cooker, lock the PRESSURE SEAL, and bring up to pressure.

5. Once done, release pressure by quick release method.

6. Stir to combine. Bring to bowls and serve with a whirl of olive oil and big chunks of bread.

Mongolian Beef

We took this traditional Asian dish and speeded it up through the power of high-pressure. What would take 40 minutes, is now ready in 15. Watch out for the salt, as the soy sauce sometimes can be heavy on sodium. And always use fresh beef steaks. Serve it with rice or noodles, and steamed vegetables.

Serves: 6
Preparation Time: 15 minutes
Cooking Time: 12 minutes

INGREDIENTS:

Salt and pepper to taste
Vegetable oil to taste
(½ tbsp) Ginger, minced
(2 tbsp) Garlic, minced
(⅔ cup) Brown sugar

(½ cup) Soy sauce
(1 cup) Water/vegetable stock
(2 cups) Onions, sliced
(2 lbs) Flank steak, strips

PREPARATION:

1. Place the beef in a baking dish.

2. Coat the beef evenly with salt and pepper to taste.

COOKING STEPS:

1. Hit MEAT/CHICKEN followed by TIME ADJUSTMENT and correct time to 12 minutes.

2. Heat the oil, sauté the beef, the onions and the garlic until and brown.

3. Add the remaining ingredients. Stir to combine.

4. Place lid on cooker, lock the PRESSURE SEAL, and bring up to pressure.

5. Once done, release pressure by quick release method.

6. Place dish over platter and serve.

Braised Beef

If you want meat falling off the bones, keep on reading. This dish takes the classic slow roast approach and adds the pressure element. It's the same juicy-tender beef, but done in only 35 minutes. Add potatoes and steamed vegetables on the side and you've got a full meal that puts everyone at home to sleep happy.

Serves: 4. 8
Preparation Time: 5 minutes
Cooking Time: 35 minutes

INGREDIENTS:

Salt and pepper to taste
Vegetable oil to taste
(2 cups) Onions, quartered

(2 tbsp) Garlic, whole
(2 cups) water/vegetable stock
(4 lbs) Beef, short ribs

PREPARATION:

1. Place the beef in a baking dish.

2. Coat the beef evenly with salt and pepper to taste.

COOKING STEPS:

1. Hit MEAT/CHICKEN followed by TIME ADJUSTMENT and correct time to 35 minutes.

2. Heat the oil, sauté the beef until brown.

3. Add the onion, the garlic and the water/stock. Stir to combine.

4. Place lid on cooker, lock the PRESSURE SEAL, and bring up to pressure.

5. Once done, release pressure by quick release method.

6. Remove bones if desired. Place dish over platter and serve.

Beef Stew

Once the winter comes, you need to absorb heat from very possible source. That's where this beef stews makes itself more than necessary. With only 35 minutes of cooking time, this dish will keep your family and friends up for the whole season. Serve it with big chunks of bread and a swirl of olive oil.

Serves: 4 - 6
Preparation Time: 5 minutes
Cooking Time: 30 minutes

INGREDIENTS:

Olive oil to taste
Salt and pepper to taste
(1 cup) Onions, sliced
(1 tbsp) Tomato paste
(2 tbsp) Bay leaves

(2 tbsp) Thyme
(2 tbsp) Garlic, whole
(2 cups) Beef broth
(3 cups) Carrots, sliced
(2 lbs) Beef stew meat, chunks

PREPARATION:

1. Place the beef in a baking dish.

2. Coat the beef evenly with salt and pepper to taste.

COOKING STEPS:

1. Hit MEAT/CHICKEN followed by TIME ADJUSTMENT and correct time to 35 minutes.

2. Heat the oil, sauté the beef until brown.

3. Add the onion, the garlic, the carrots, the herbs and the broth. Stir to combine.

4. Place lid on cooker, lock the PRESSURE SEAL, and bring up to pressure.

5. Once done, release pressure by quick release method.

6. Stir it well and serve it directly from the pot.

Mexican Beef

The taste of a slow roast with the smoothness of a stew. The Mexicans invented it but the French took it over. Within 35 minutes, you can easily get it done and transform a sad dinner into a legendary party. Serve it with rice, tortillas, wraps, salads, sour cream, tomato-salsa and guacamole.

Serves: 4 - 6
Preparation Time: 15 minutes
Cooking Time: 35 minutes

INGREDIENTS:

Salt and pepper to taste
Vegetable oil to taste
(1 tbsp) Chili powder
(1 cup) Onions, sliced
(1 tbsp) tomato paste
(3 tbsp) Garlic, smashed

(½ cup) tomato salsa
(½ cup) Beef broth
(½ cup) Cilantro, minced
(2 ½ lbs) Beef short ribs, brisket, or chuck roast, boneless, cubes

PREPARATION:

1. Place the beef in a baking dish.

2. Coat the beef evenly with salt, pepper and chilli to taste.

COOKING STEPS:

1. Hit MEAT/CHICKEN followed by TIME ADJUSTMENT and correct time to 35 minutes.

2. Heat the oil, sauté the beef until brown.

3. Add the onion, the garlic, the tomato and the broth. Stir to combine.

4. Place lid on cooker, lock the PRESSURE SEAL, and bring up to pressure.

5. Once done, release pressure by slow release method.

6. Stir it well and serve it directly from the pot. Add cilantro as desired.

Ossobuco

That's the veal shank, now celebrated by chefs and TV shows as the greatest thing ever. Cook it under high-pressure for 60 minutes and it will be tender enough to be served with the meat falling off the bone. Remember to pour the meat juicy juiciness over the dish. Serve it with mashed potatoes and steamed vegetables for a healthy bonus.

Serves: 4 - 6
Preparation Time: 10 minutes
Cooking Time: 60 minutes

INGREDIENTS:

Salt and pepper to taste
Olive oil to taste
(2 tbsp) Thyme
(2 tbsp) Garlic, minced
(½ cup) Lemon, juiced
(1 cup) Celery, chopped
(1 cup) Onions, chopped

(2 cups) Flour, wheat is fine
(1 cup) Parsley
(1 cup) Beef stock
(½ cup) Dry red wine
(1 cup) Tomatoes, diced
(2 cups) Carrots, chopped
(3 lbs) Veal shanks, whole

PREPARATION:

1. In a bowl, mix the garlic, the parsley and the lemon and reserve.

COOKING STEPS:

1. Hit CANNING/PRESERVING followed by TIME ADJUSTMENT and correct time to 60 minutes.

2. Heat the oil in the pot. Add the veal shanks. Season and sauté every possible side until brown. Remove the meat and reserve.

3. Add the vegetables and the herbs. Starting with the onions, stir gradually with the wine. Brown until carrots are golden.

4. Bring the veal shanks back. Add the water and stir to combine. Season to taste.

5. Place lid on cooker, lock the PRESSURE SEAL, and bring up to pressure.

6. Once done, release pressure by slow release method, letting the steam escape naturally.

7. Bring the dish to a platter and serve with the lemon-garlic-parsley sauce on the side.

Lamb Broccoli Stew

Families were born because of this dish. So let's show some respect and cook it with the freshest ingredients. The broccoli sides with the lamb perfectly in a dark and gravy soup. The rosemary and the thyme, once and again, meet to make meat right. This deliciousness needs only 60 minutes under high-pressure to get boiled down to a sauce of heavens. Serve it with steamed vegetables, mashed potatoes or rice.

Serves: 3 to 6
Preparation Time: 10 minutes
Cooking Time: 65 minutes

INGREDIENTS:

Vegetable oil to taste
(2 tbsp) Garlic, chopped
(1 tbsp) Rosemary
(1 tbsp) Thyme
(1 tbsp) Bay leaf

(1 cup) Dry white wine
(3 cups) Onions, chopped
(3 cups) Broccoli, chunks, cooked/steamed
(8 cups) Vegetable broth
(3 lbs) Bone-in lamb shoulder, chunks

COOKING STEPS:

1. Hit CANNING/PRESERVING followed by TIME ADJUSTMENT and correct time to 60 minutes.

2. Heat the oil in the pot. Add lamb, the onion, the garlic and the herbs. Season and sauté every possible side of the meat. Gradually pour in the white wine. Stir until brown.

3. Add the water/stock and stir to combine. Season to taste.

4. Place lid on cooker, lock the PRESSURE SEAL, and bring up to pressure.

5. Once done, release pressure by slow release method, letting the steam escape naturally.

6. Add in the broccoli and stir to combine. Close the lid and let the remaining heat cook the broccoli for more 5 minutes.

6. Remove bones if desired. Bring the dish to a bowl and serve.

Vitello Tonnato

A whole veal roast braised under pressure. It cooks splendidly with the vegetables, creating a sauce that should be saved for generations. This Italian dish is beyond the entree menu, serving also as the main guest in a delicious sandwich. And don't forget to try the easy-to-do mayo and tuna sauce for the classic antipasti taste.

Serves: 4 - 5
Preparation Time: 5 minutes
Cooking Time: 25 minutes

INGREDIENTS:

Olive oil to taste
Salt and pepper to taste
(2 tbsp) Rosemary
(2 tbsp) Garlic, chopped
(1 cup) Onions, diced

(1 cup) Carrots, diced
(1 cup) Celery, diced
(1 cup) Vegetable stock
(1 cup) White wine, dry
(1 ½ lbs) Veal roast, whole

Sauce:

Mayo (1 cup)

Tuna, canned (3 oz)

PREPARATION:

1. In a bowl, mix the mayo and the tuna. Reserve.

COOKING STEPS:

1. Hit MEAT/CHICKEN followed by TIME ADJUSTMENT and correct time to 25 minutes.

2. Heat the oil and brown the veal, the onions and the garlic. Season to taste.

3. Add carrots, celery, the stock, the rosemary and the wine. Stir to combine.

4. Place lid on cooker, lock the PRESSURE SEAL, and bring up to pressure.

5. Once done, release pressure by quick release method.

6. Let the dish cool down and bring it to the fridge. Cut the meat in slices and serve as antipasti with the tuna-mayo sauce.

SEAFOOD

Paella

Ah, the Spanish Paella. A classic all-day-cooking dish now done in 35 minutes. Under high-pressure, the rice will merge tastes with the meat and spices. The seafood at the end becomes the grand finale. Aim for the freshest of the shrimps and clams and you will barely need to cook them. Perfect for parties and family gatherings.

Serves: 4 - 6
Preparation Time: 15 minutes
Cooking Time: 35 minutes

INGREDIENTS:

Salt and pepper to taste
Olive oil to taste
(¼ tbsp) Marjoram, dry
(¼ tbsp) Cumin, powder
(⅛ tbsp) Whole saffron, dry
(1 tbsp) Cloves garlic, minced
(3 tbsp) Lemon, wedged
(1 cup) Onions, diced

(½ cup) Green peas
(3 cups) Chicken stock
(8 oz) Spicy chorizo sausage, slices
(15 oz) Long-grain rice, uncooked
(½ lbs) Whole shrimp, headless
(½ lbs) Clams, in the shell, drained
(1 lb) Chicken breast, boneless, diced

PREPARATION:

1. Place the chicken in a baking dish.

2. Coat the chicken evenly with salt and pepper to taste.

COOKING STEPS:

1. Hit MEAT/CHICKEN followed by TIME ADJUSTMENT and correct time to 20 minutes.

2. Heat the oil, sauté the chicken and the chorizo until well cooked.

3. Add the rice, the garlic, the green peas, the spices and the stock. Stir to combine.

4. Place lid on cooker, lock the PRESSURE SEAL, and bring up to pressure.

5. Once done, release pressure by quick release method.

6. Add the shrimps and the clams. Stir to combine.

7. Place the lid once again on cooker and let the remaining heat cook the seafood for 5 to 10 minutes. (the shrimps should be tender and opaque and the clams should be opened).

8. Stir it well. Place dish over platter and serve.

Coconut Shrimp

Such a simple recipe, this is presumably the first dish invented by men. And it survives deliciously until now. Here, we make it in 12 minutes with a recipe that can be easily followed in a cabin kitchen. Search for the freshest of the shrimps and get that fishing village restaurant taste.

Serves: 6 to 8
Preparation Time: 5 minutes
Cooking Time: 12 minutes

INGREDIENTS:

Salt and pepper to taste
Vegetable oil to taste
(2 tbsp) Ginger, chopped
(2 tbsp) Garlic, chopped
(½ cup) Cilantro, chopped

(1 cup) Onion, chopped
(1 cup) Coconut milk
(2 cups) Carrots, diced
(3 cups) Fish broth
(2 lbs) Shrimp, peeled

COOKING STEPS:

1. Hit FISH/VEGETABLE/STEAM followed by TIME ADJUSTMENT and correct time to 12 minutes.

2. Heat the oil, sauté the shrimp and the ginger briefly. Season to taste and reserve.

3. Add vegetables and herbs to the pot. Sauté until the onions are brown. Pour in the fish broth and stir to combine.

4. Place lid on cooker, lock the PRESSURE SEAL, and bring up to pressure.

5. Once done, release pressure by quick release method.

6. Add coconut milk and shrimps. Stir to combine. Serve soup in bowls as entree along rice or noodles.

Cioppino

This Italian take on seafood soup doesn't fail. In 8 minutes the clams, the scallops and the shrimps will dance with the tomato in a boiling ballroom of tastes that only poetry could really describe it. It's the perfect entree for masquerade dinner parties and family reunions.

Serves: 5 - 6
Preparation Time: 5 minutes
Cooking Time: 8 minutes

INGREDIENTS:

Salt and pepper to taste
Olive oil to taste
(2 tbsp) Garlic, chopped
(½ cup) Cilantro, chopped
(1 cup) Onion, chopped
(1 cup) White dry wine

(2 cups) Green bell pepper, diced
(2 cups) Tomatoes, diced
(3 cups) Fish broth
(1 lb) Shrimp, peeled
(½ lb) Scallops, quartered
(1 lb) Clams, scrubbed

COOKING STEPS:

1. Hit FISH/VEGETABLE/STEAM followed by TIME ADJUSTMENT and correct time to 8 minutes.

2. Heat the oil, sauté the garlic, the onion and the peppers until brown.

3. Add tomatoes and white wine. Stir to deglaze. Pour in fish broth and stir to combine.

4. Place lid on cooker, lock the PRESSURE SEAL, and bring up to pressure.

5. Once done, release pressure by quick release method.

6. Add the seafood. Gently stir to combine. Let it cook under the remaining heat until shrimps are tender and clams are open. Serve it as entree for fish or pasta.

Mediterranean Fish

One of the fastest recipes in this book. Follow it and lunch will be done in less than 15 minutes. The fish gets so well cooked, it will dissolve mouths and awkward family moments. The spices will trigger memories from fishing villages and perfect family lunches under the sun. Serve it with white wine for the grown-ups and take the rest of the day off - it's the siesta and you deserve it!

Serves: 4
Preparation Time: 5 minutes
Cooking Time: 8 minutes

INGREDIENTS:

Olive Oil to taste
Salt and pepper to taste
(1 tbsp) Garlic, minced
(2 tbsp) Pickled capers

(2 tbsp) Thyme
(1 cup) Black olives
(1 lb) Cherry tomatoes, halves
(1 ½ lbs) White fish fillets, cod works great

COOKING STEPS:

1. Place the steamer tray in the pot. Add 1 to 2 cups of water.

2. Add the fish, the tomatoes, the thyme, the capers, the olives and the garlic carefully over the tray. Make it sure the ingredients are just above the water level. Season to taste.

3. Hit FISH/VEGETABLE/STEAM followed by TIME ADJUSTMENT and correct time to 8 minutes.

4. Place lid on cooker, lock the PRESSURE SEAL, and bring up to pressure.

5. Once done, release pressure by quick release method.

6. Serve it in each plate individually.

Coconut Curry Fish

Test the limits of your family palpable senses. The wild starchy coconut simmers the fish in a symmetry of tastes and compliments. The flagrant curry after-taste reminds us to drink more water. Done in remarkable 10 minutes in total, it goes perfect with Jasmine rice and steamed vegetables.

Serves: 4 - 6
Preparation Time: 5 minutes
Cooking Time: 5 minutes

INGREDIENTS:

Vegetable oil to taste
Salt and pepper to taste
Lemon juice to taste
(1 tbsp) Ginger, grated
(2 tbsp) Garlic, crushed
(2 tbsp) Green Chilies, strips

(3 tbsp) Curry, powder
(2 cups) Onions, strips
(1 cup) Tomato, chopped
(2 cups) Coconut milk
(1 ½ lbs) Fish steaks or fillets, strips

COOKING STEPS:

1. Hit FISH/VEGETABLE/STEAM followed by TIME ADJUSTMENT and correct time to 5 minutes.

2. Heat the oil, sauté the garlic, the ginger and the onions until brown.

3. Add salt, the spices and the coconut milk. Stir to combine.

4. Gently add the tomatoes, the chiles and the fish.

5. Place lid on cooker, lock the PRESSURE SEAL, and bring up to pressure.

6. Once done, release pressure by quick release method.

7. Serve in individual plates. Add lemon juice to taste.

One Pot Tuna Pasta

Introducing the ultimate last resource dinner. The gourmet of the dark end of the cupboard. This dish can be done using only processed foods, those ingredients we always have lost somewhere in our kitchen. It serves well for the student houses and the families hibernating through the winter.

Serves: 4 - 6
Preparation Time: 1 minute
Cooking Time: 5 minutes

INGREDIENTS:

Salt and pepper to taste
Parmesan cheese to taste
Olive oil to taste
(1 tbsp) Garlic, crushed
(2 tbsp) Capers, pickled
(¼ cup) Thyme, dry

(2 cups) Tomato puree
(3 oz) 3 anchovies filets, crushed
(5 ½ oz) Canned tuna in olive oil
(2 cups) Water
(16 oz) Dry pasta, fusilli and penne work great

COOKING STEPS:

1. Hit FISH/VEGETABLE/STEAM followed by TIME ADJUSTMENT and correct time to 5 minutes.

2. Heat the oil, sauté the garlic and the anchovies briefly.

3. Add the tomato puree, the pasta and the tuna. Salt to taste. Stir to combine.

4. Add water (enough to cover the pasta)

5. Place lid on cooker, lock the PRESSURE SEAL, and bring up to pressure.

6. Once done, release pressure by quick release method.

7. Stir it well. Place dish over platter and serve with parmesan cheese.

Mussels Marinara

Sea pearls cooked under the Mediterranean juice of the tomatoes. It doesn't get much better than this. Make your own self made sauce marinara and bring it in for a spectacular upgrade from the canned tomatoes. It serves amazingly well as the sauce for a linguini.

Serves: 4
Preparation Time: 2 minutes
Cooking Time: 4 minutes

INGREDIENTS:

Salt and pepper to taste
Olive oil to taste
(1 tbsp) Basil
(2 tbsp) Garlic, crushed

(½ cup) Parsley, chopped
(1 cup) Dry white wine
(28 oz) Tomatoes, crushed
(3 lbs) Mussels, scrubbed

COOKING STEPS:

1. Hit FISH/VEGETABLE/STEAM followed by TIME ADJUSTMENT and correct time to 4 minutes.

2. Heat the oil, sauté the garlic and the spices briefly.

3. Add the wine, the tomatoes and the mussels. Season to taste. Gently stir to combine.

5. Place lid on cooker, lock the PRESSURE SEAL, and bring up to pressure.

6. Once done, release pressure by quick release method.

7. Add parsley and remove the unopened shells. Transfer it to a bowl and serve it.

Bouillabaisse

A dash of this French seafood stew could sustain families through whole winters. This classic recipe now boils up in quick 8 minutes under high-pressure, blinking easily into your evening routine. It's a classic entree dish for elegant dinners, followed by extravagant roasts and remembered by legendary guests.

Serves: 4 - 6
Preparation Time: 5 minutes
Cooking Time: 4 minutes

INGREDIENTS:

Olive oil to taste
Salt and pepper to taste
(2 tbsp) Garlic, crushed
(2 tbsp) Parsley, chopped
(1 tbsp) Bay leaves
(1 tbsp) Thyme
(¼ tbsp) Saffron, crushed
(2 cups) Onions, chopped

(4 cups) Water/vegetable stock
(6 oz) 6 clams in shells
(8 oz) Tomatoes, crushed
(12 oz) Scallops
(¼ lb) Shrimp, shelled
(1 lb) Lobster tail, chunks
(1 lb) White fish fillets, cod works great, chunks

COOKING STEPS:

1. Hit FISH/VEGETABLE/STEAM followed by TIME ADJUSTMENT and correct time to 5 minutes.

2. Heat the oil, sauté the garlic, the onions and the herbs briefly.

3. Add the tomatoes and the water/stock. Season to taste. Stir to combine.

4. Place lid on cooker, lock the PRESSURE SEAL, and bring up to pressure.

5. Once done, release pressure by quick release method.

6. Add the fish and seafood and stir gently. Hit FISH/VEGETABLE/STEAM again followed by TIME ADJUSTMENT and correct time to 3 minutes.

7. Place lid on cooker, lock the PRESSURE SEAL, and bring up to pressure.

8. Once done, release pressure by quick release method.

9. Transfer it to a bowl and serve it.

STARTERS AND SIDE DISHES

Onion Soup

That's basically why the French invented the pressure cooker. This dish could take up to 4 hours in the original stove top recipe. But here, you get caramelized onion soup under 30 minutes. Top the bowl with a melted cheese toast and serve it just like the French would.

Serves: 4 - 5
Preparation Time: 10 minutes
Cooking Time: 30 minutes

INGREDIENTS:

Salt and pepper to taste
Butter to taste
(1 tbsp) Thyme, dry
(1 tbsp) Rosemary, dry

(2 tbsp) Bay leaves
(½ cup) Dry sherry
(8 cups) Chicken stock
(3 lbs) Onions, slices

COOKING STEPS:

1. Hit CANNING/PRESERVING followed by TIME ADJUSTMENT and correct time to 20 minutes.

2. Heat the butter, add the onions and sauté until brown. Slowly pour in the sherry. Season to taste.

3. Add remaining ingredients. Stir to combine.

4. Place lid on cooker, lock the PRESSURE SEAL, and bring up to pressure.

5. Once done, release pressure by quick release method.

6. Stir to combine. Bring to bowls and serve with a toast and melted cheese on top.

Broccoli Cheese Soup

This dish is such a modern classic, even fast food chains are serving it by now. But here you take all the credits by making your own soup from scratch. In only 15 minutes you can have the delicious mixture of the healthy broccoli and the sinful cheese. Yummy!

Serves: 4 - 5
Preparation Time: 10 minutes
Cooking Time: 15 minutes

INGREDIENTS:

Salt and pepper to taste
Butter to taste
(1 tbsp) Thyme, dry
(1 tbsp) Rosemary, dry
(2 tbsp) Garlic, crushed

(2 cups) Vegetable stock
(1 cup) Milk
(2 cups) Cheese, cheddar works amazingly, grated
(6 cups) Broccoli, chopped

COOKING STEPS:

1. Hit CANNING/PRESERVING followed by TIME ADJUSTMENT and correct time to 15 minutes.

2. Heat the butter and sauté the garlic until brown. Add the herbs, the broccoli, the milk and the stock. Stir to combine.

3. Place lid on cooker, lock the PRESSURE SEAL, and bring up to pressure.

4. Once done, release pressure by slow release method, letting the steam escape naturally.

5. Add cheese and stir to combine. Bring dish to blender or food processor for creamy consistency. Transfer to bowls and serve it along big chunks of bread.

Tomato Soup

The most famous soup can ever, here it takes a turn for the best. In 5 minutes you get a taste and an aroma that no ready-meal could ever bring to your table. Serve it with fresh basil on top just to remind everyone that homemade meals will prevail in your house.

Serves: 4 - 5
Preparation Time: 10 minutes
Cooking Time: 5 minutes

INGREDIENTS:

Salt and pepper to taste
Olive oil to taste
(1 tbsp) Thyme, dry
(2 tbsp) Garlic, crushed
(¼ cup) Basil, fresh
(1 cup) Celery, diced

(1 cup) Carrots, diced
(2 cups) Cheese, parmesan works amazingly, grated
(2 cups) Vegetable stock
(3 lbs) Tomato, peeled, seeded, quartered

COOKING STEPS:

1. Hit BEANS/LENTILS followed by TIME ADJUSTMENT and correct time to 5 minutes.

2. Heat the oil, sauté the garlic, the onions, the celery and the carrots. Season to taste.

3. Add the stock, the tomatoes and herbs. Stir to combine.

4. Place lid on cooker, lock the PRESSURE SEAL, and bring up to pressure.

5. Once done, release pressure by quick release method.

6. Add cheese and stir to combine. Bring dish to blender or food processor for creamy consistency. Transfer to bowls and serve it along big chunks of bread, cream and a swirl of olive oil.

Moroccan Lentils

This delicious recipe comes from Africa directly to your table with a short stop at your pressure cooker. In 20 minutes, the lentils become soft and juicy, gathering the fresh taste and aroma from the vegetables. Ah, the saffron is a must, so don't forget it!

Serves: 4 - 5
Preparation Time: 5 minutes
Cooking Time: 20 minutes

INGREDIENTS:

Olive oil to taste.
Salt and pepper to taste.
(½ tbsp) Saffron, ground
(½ tbsp) Ginger, ground
(½ cup) Parsley, chopped

(1 cup) Onions, diced
(1 cup) Carrots, diced
(1 cup) Celery, diced
(1 cup) Lentils, rinsed
(5 cups) Vegetable stock

COOKING STEPS:

1. Hit MEAT/CHICKEN followed by TIME ADJUSTMENT and correct time to 20 minutes.

2. Heat the oil and brown the onions, the carrots and the celery. Season to taste.

3. Add the lentils, the spices and the stock. Stir to combine.

4. Place lid on cooker, lock the PRESSURE SEAL, and bring up to pressure.

5. Once done, release pressure by quick release method.

6. Transfer to bowls and serve with rice.

Mac'n Cheese

America's favorite side dish, now done in unbelievable 5 minutes. Wow. Experiment with different types of cheese and pasta. Serve it along poultry or beef. There's not much to add to make this dish better - and that's definitely a compliment.

Serves: 4 - 5
Preparation Time: 10 minutes
Cooking Time: 5 minutes

INGREDIENTS:

Salt and pepper to taste
Butter to taste
(1 tbsp) Oregano, dry
(1 cup) Milk

(2 cups) Cheese, parmesan works amazingly, grated
(3 cups) Vegetable stock
(1 lb) Dry pasta

COOKING STEPS:

1. Hit BEANS/LENTILS followed by TIME ADJUSTMENT and correct time to 5 minutes.

2. Add every ingredient to the pot (besides the cheese and butter) and stir to combine. Season to taste.

3. Place lid on cooker, lock the PRESSURE SEAL, and bring up to pressure.

4. Once done, release pressure by quick release method.

5. Add butter and cheese and stir to combine. Transfer to bowls and serve it as a classic side dish for meat.

Borscht

This fragrant beetroot soup travelled all the way from east Europe to end up at your taste buds. The beautiful dark red color asks for a spoon of cream, and the fresh parsley joins in for a mix of tastes that will make you wish for a bigger bowl. What a trip!

Serves: 4 - 5
Preparation Time: 10 minutes
Cooking Time: 5 minutes

INGREDIENTS:

Salt and pepper to taste
Butter to taste
(1 tbsp) Oregano, dry
(2 tbsp) Garlic,
(1 cup) Onions, diced

(2 cups) Potatoes, diced
(2 cups) Carrots, diced
(3 cups) Vegetable stock
(3 lb) Beets, cooked, diced

COOKING STEPS:

1. Hit BEANS/LENTILS followed by TIME ADJUSTMENT and correct time to 10 minutes.

2. Heat the butter, add the onions, the garlic, the potatoes and the carrots. Season to taste. Sauté until brown.

3. Add the remaining ingredients and stir to combine.

4. Place lid on cooker, lock the PRESSURE SEAL, and bring up to pressure.

5. Once done, release pressure by quick release method.

6. Stir to combine. Transfer to bowls and serve it with fresh parsley and fresh cream.

Ginger Carrot Soup

This prominent entree goes well with anything. It's the friend of every dish, taking part in lunches, dinners and banquets, serving tables along meat, fruits and salads. Add a pinch of fresh ginger for that unique aroma and remind everyone that healthy can be tasty.

Serves: 4 - 5
Preparation Time: 10 minutes
Cooking Time: 15 minutes

INGREDIENTS:

Salt and pepper to taste
Butter to taste
(1 tbsp) Thyme, dry
(2 tbsp) Garlic, crushed
(2 tbsp) Ginger, ground

(3 cups) Onions, diced
(2 cups) Potatoes, diced
(3 cups) Vegetable stock
(6 cups) Carrots, diced

COOKING STEPS:

1. Hit BEANS/LENTILS followed by TIME ADJUSTMENT and correct time to 15 minutes.

2. Heat the butter, add the onions, the garlic, the potatoes and the carrots. Season to taste. Sauté until brown.

3. Add the remaining ingredients and stir to combine.

4. Place lid on cooker, lock the PRESSURE SEAL, and bring up to pressure.

5. Once done, release pressure by quick release method.

6. Remove dish to blender or food processor and reduce it to a creamy liquid paste. Transfer to bowls and serve it with more fresh ground ginger and fresh cream.

Fastest White Rice Ever

That's the easiest way to learn how to rice. Cooking under 5 minutes in high-pressure, this delicious white plain side dish will be an easy add-on to almost every meal. Keep it ready for Asian and latin flavored recipes. Add your favorite herbs to spice it up and you can call it yours.

Serves: 4 - 5
Preparation Time: 1 minute
Cooking Time: 4 minutes

INGREDIENTS:

Salt and pepper to taste
Vegetable oil to taste

(2 cups) White rice
(3 cups) Vegetable stock

COOKING STEPS:

1. Add every ingredient to the pot and stir to combine. Depending on the broth, just a pinch of salt will be enough to season it.

2. Hit VEGETABLE/FISH/STEAM followed by TIME ADJUSTMENT and correct time to 4 minutes.

3. Place lid on cooker, lock the PRESSURE SEAL, and bring up to pressure.

4. Once done, release pressure by slow release method, letting the steam escape naturally.

5. Transfer dish to a bowl and serve along almost every dish in history of cooking.

Vegan Tofu Frittata

The vegans are taking over the world, so let's score some points with them. Here, we learn how to replace eggs with tofu in a delicious frittata that balances colors and flavors amazingly well. But be aware: it requires some preparation work. Who said eating healthy and ethically would be easy?

Serves: 4
Preparation Time: 10 minute
Cooking Time: 15 minutes

INGREDIENTS:

Salt and pepper to taste
Vegetable oil to taste
(1 tbsp) Thyme, dry
(1 tbsp) Parsley, chopped
(1 tbsp) Garlic, crushed
(1 tbsp) Yeast, dry
(½ cup) Vegetable milk, rice or soy

(½ cup) Flour, wheat/corn
(1 cup) Onion, chopped
(1 cup) Zucchini, sliced
(1 cup) Potatoes, diced
(3 cups) Vegetable stock
(2 cups) Tofu, ground

PREPARATION:

1. In a blender or food processor, bring the tofu, the vegetable milk and the flour. Blend it to a liquid dough, just like pancake batter. Season to taste and reserve.

COOKING STEPS:

1. Hit VEGETABLE/FISH/STEAM followed by TIME ADJUSTMENT and correct time to 15 minutes.

2. Place lid on cooker, lock the PRESSURE SEAL, and bring up to pressure.

3. Once done, release pressure by slow release method, letting the steam escape naturally.

4. Cut frittata in pies or mix for scrambled tofu. Serve with a side of salad for lunch or toast for breakfast.

Steamed Vegetables

Probably the easiest recipe in any cooking book. Add the water, cut the vegetables, close the lid, done. You can add your own taste with a pinch of your favorite spice and herb as you serve. It goes tremendously well with everything: pork, lamb, beef, rice, pasta, salt and pepper.

Serves: 4 - 5
Preparation Time: 5 minutes
Cooking Time: 8 minutes

INGREDIENTS:

Salt and pepper to taste
Vegetable oil to taste
(1 tbsp) Thyme, dry
(1 tbsp) Parsley, chopped
(1 tbsp) Garlic, diced
(1 cup) Celery, sliced

(1 cup) Red bell pepper, sliced
(2 cups) Zucchini, sliced
(2 cups) Carrots, sliced
(2 cups) Potatoes, diced
(4 cups) Water

COOKING STEPS:

1. Add STEAM TRAY to the pot and pour the water it. Add all the ingredients and make sure they are not soaked in water.

2. Hit VEGETABLE/FISH/STEAM followed by TIME ADJUSTMENT and correct time to 8 minutes.

3. Place lid on cooker, lock the PRESSURE SEAL, and bring up to pressure.

4. Once done, release pressure by quick release method.

5. Bring vegetables to a bowl. Serve with extra seasoning and olive oil. It's a great side dish for almost every meal in this book.

Potato Soup

This delicious recipe is embalmed in every cooking book. Here we bring a fast and simple version of this amazing soup that asks for your own final touches. Let everyone at home customize their toppings and transform this meal into a party. It goes great with fresh herbs in summer lunches, or with bacon and cheese in winter feasts.

Serves: 4 - 5
Preparation Time: 1 minute
Cooking Time: 30 minutes

INGREDIENTS:

Salt and pepper to taste
Vegetable oil to taste
(1 tbsp) Parsley, chopped
(1 tbsp) Garlic, crushed
(1 cup) Onions, diced

(1 cup) Celery, sliced
(2 cups) Carrots, sliced
(4 cups) Vegetable stock
(3 lbs) Potatoes, chunks

COOKING STEPS:

1. Hit CANNING/PRESERVING followed by TIME ADJUSTMENT and correct time to 30 minutes.

2. Heat the oil, sauté all the vegetables briefly. Season to taste. As the onions gets browner, add the stock.

3. Place lid on cooker, lock the PRESSURE SEAL, and bring up to pressure.

4. Once done, release pressure by quick release method.

5. Bring vegetables to a blender or food processor. Blend it and slowly pour water from the pot to adjust the consistency. Once the potato becomes a creamy pasty soup, bring it to bowls and top it with fresh parsley.

Cuban Black Beans

It all starts with a delicious sofrito, a classic mirepoix of green peppers, onions and garlic. This mixture layers flavors and aromas throughout the whole dish, making the beans taste like a meal from paradise. Serve it along rice and salad for an authentic Caribbean banquet.

Serves: 4 - 5
Preparation Time: 5 minutes (+12 hours for beans to soak)
Cooking Time: 25 minutes

INGREDIENTS:

Salt and pepper to taste
Olive oil to taste
(2 tbsp) Bay leaves
(2 tbsp) Garlic, minced
(½ cup) Cilantro, chopped

(1 cup) Green bell peppers, chopped
(1 cup) Onions, chopped
(2 cups) Black beans, soaked
(3 cups) Vegetable broth

PREPARATION:

1. In a bowl, let the beans soaking in water overnight. Rinse them before cooking.

COOKING STEPS:

1. Hit CANNING/PRESERVING followed by TIME ADJUSTMENT and correct time to 25 minutes.

2. Heat the oil, sauté the green peppers, the onions and the garlic until brown.

3. Add the beans, the herbs and the stock. Season to taste. Stir to combine.

4. Place lid on cooker, lock the PRESSURE SEAL, and bring up to pressure.

5. Once done, release pressure by slow release method, letting the steam escape naturally.

6. Bring the beans to a bowl and serve along rice, salad and meat.

Tomato Risotto

Here we change the rules of cooking and prepare this marvelous tomato risotto without the constant stirring of the rice. What a sacrilege! But don't worry, this classic Italian meal can be easily approved without the traditions. Let the high-pressure do all the work. Our job here is to eat it, anyway.

Serves: 4 - 5
Preparation Time: 5 minutes
Cooking Time: 5 minutes

INGREDIENTS:

Salt and pepper to taste
Olive oil to taste
(1 tbsp) Thyme, dry
(1 tbsp) Oregano, dry
(2 tbsp) Garlic, minced

(1 cup) Onions, chopped
(2 cups) Rice, arborio
(3 cups) Tomatoes, diced
(3 cups) Vegetable broth

COOKING STEPS:

1. Hit FISH/VEGETABLE/STEAM followed by TIME ADJUSTMENT and correct time to 5 minutes.

2. Heat the oil, sauté the onions, the garlic and the tomatoes briefly.

3. Add the rice, the herbs and the stock. Season to taste. Stir to combine.

4. Place lid on cooker, lock the PRESSURE SEAL, and bring up to pressure.

5. Once done, release pressure by slow release method, letting the steam escape naturally.

6. Bring the rice to a bowl and serve with a top of parmesan cheese and swirl of olive oil.

Corn On The Cob

All it takes is 2 minutes to make corn melt butter and hearts. This side dish can easily steal the show when served hot and fresh. Salt and pepper are the only requirements of this delicious dish that doesn't need much to be tasty.

Serves: 3 - 4
Preparation Time: 1 minute
Cooking Time: 2 minutes

INGREDIENTS:

Salt and pepper to taste
Butter to taste

(3 cups) Corn ears, whole
(3 cups) Water

COOKING STEPS:

1. Add STEAM TRAY to the pot. Pour in the water and place the corn in.

2. Hit FISH/VEGETABLE/STEAM followed by TIME ADJUSTMENT and correct time to 2 minutes.

3. Place lid on cooker, lock the PRESSURE SEAL, and bring up to pressure.

4. Once done, release pressure by quick release method.

5. Bring the corn to plate and season to taste. Add butter immediately to melt and serve.

High-Pressure Ratatouille

Hollywood made it famous, but we speeded it up through the power of high-pressure. It's true you won't get that crispy overlayer brought by the oven. But, just like in every other dish, the Ratatouille becomes a new thing once cooked under high-pressure. In 5 minutes the freshest oregano, the soft eggplant and the juicy tomatoes slices will prove you that there's more than one way of cooking anything.

Serves: 4 - 5
Preparation Time: 5 minutes
Cooking Time: 5 minutes

INGREDIENTS:

Salt and pepper to taste
Olive oil to taste
(1 tbsp) Oregano, dry
(2 tbsp) Basil, chopped
(2 tbsp) Garlic, chopped

(1 cup) Onions, sliced
(2 cups) Tomatoes, diced
(2 cups) Zucchini, sliced
(3 cups) Eggplant, sliced

COOKING STEPS:

1. Hit FISH/VEGETABLE/STEAM followed by TIME ADJUSTMENT and correct time to 5 minutes.

2. Heat the oil and sauté the vegetables and the herbs briefly. Season to taste.

3. Place lid on cooker, lock the PRESSURE SEAL, and bring up to pressure.

4. Once done, release pressure by quick release method.

5. Bring dish to bowl and serve along rice, fish or meat.

Polenta

Kneaded easily by butter and salt, this smooth and succulent puree is the perfect side dish for fish and meats, cobs and lambs, steaks and shrimps. Together with salad, it forms the triumvirate of the modern Italian dinner. Save the leftovers and make great side dishes. Deep fry them in polenta sticks, or make a simple oven-baked polenta with tomato sauce and cheese.

Serves: 4 - 6
Preparation Time: 5 minutes
Cooking Time: 4 minutes

INGREDIENTS:

Salt to taste
(2 cups) Coarse polenta corn flour, bramata
(8 cups) Water, broth, or a mix of water and milk

COOKING STEPS:

1. Hit SOUP/STEW followed by TIME ADJUSTMENT and correct time to 8 minutes.

2. Add the liquid, the salt and bring it to a boil.

3. Add the flour little by little as you stir constantly, preferably to a single direction.

4. Place lid on cooker, lock the PRESSURE SEAL, and bring up to pressure.

5. Once done, release pressure by quick release method.

6. Place the polenta on a platter and serve it with butter. Let it cool down in the fridge and make sticks for frying. Or layer it like a lasanha for baking.

Baba Ganoush

The dish of the pampered dad, the meal of the sultan. This entree is one of the central pillars of Arabian cuisine. The eggplant becomes a paste and the tahini holds everything together in a dish that has fashioned uncountable restaurants, chefs and fans. The dash of lemon makes it fresh enough to be served in the mornings along bread and a few drops of olive oil.

Serves: 6 - 8
Preparation Time: 5 minutes
Cooking Time: 5 minutes

INGREDIENTS:

Salt and pepper to taste
Olive oil to taste
(1 tbsp) Tahini
(2 tbsp) Basil, chopped

(2 tbsp) Garlic, chopped
(2 tbsp) Thyme
(¼ cup) Lemon, juiced
(3 lbs) Eggplant, peeled, chunks

COOKING STEPS:

1. Hit FISH/VEGETABLE/STEAM followed by TIME ADJUSTMENT and correct time to 5 minutes.

2. Heat the oil, sauté the eggplant and the garlic briefly. Season to taste.

3. Place lid on cooker, lock the PRESSURE SEAL, and bring up to pressure.

4. Once done, release pressure by quick release method.

5. Add tahini and lemon. Stir to combine. Bring dish to bowl and let it cool down. Serve as dip for snacks or bread spread for breakfast.

Creamy Carrot Soup

Hmm, vitamin D never tasted so good. This is the kind of dish that makes spouses leave work early. Replace cream for coconut milk and make it vegan. Batch cook it and you can save little bits of sun for 3 - 4 days in your fridge, 6 months in the freezer!

Serves: 8. 10
Preparation Time: 10 minutes
Cooking Time: 10 minutes

INGREDIENTS:

Butter to taste
Salt and pepper to taste
(½ tbsp) Mild curry powder
(4 tbsp) Garlic, crushed
(1 cup) Potatoes, peeled and diced
(1 cup) Onions, chopped

(1 ½ cup) Celery, chopped
(2 ½ cups) Onions, diced
(4 cups) Heavy whipping cream
(6 cups) Carrots, slices
(10 cups) Vegetable stock

COOKING STEPS:

1. Hit SOUP/STEW followed by TIME ADJUSTMENT and correct time to 10 minutes.

2. Melt the butter, sauté the onions, the celery and the garlic until brown.

3. Add the potatoes, the carrots, the spices and the stock. Stir to combine.

4. Place lid on cooker, lock the PRESSURE SEAL, and bring up to pressure.

5. Once done, release pressure by quick release method.

6. Add cream and transfer dish to a blender or food processor to get it completely smooth.

7. Bring it to bowl and serve it.

Red Pepper Soup

The red bell peppers become the bed for the tomatoes as their colors and tastes merge down to one delicious aroma. Don't be afraid of adding your own herbs and condiments. But be careful, this is the kind of dish that makes guests appear. Serve it with a spoon of heavy cream and croutons.

Serves: 4 - 6
Preparation Time: 7 minutes
Cooking Time: 15 minutes

INGREDIENTS:

Olive oil to taste
Salt and pepper to taste
(2 tbsp) Garlic, minced
(1 cup) Potatoes, peeled, diced
(1 cup) Dry white wine

(1 ½ cups) Onions, slices
(2 cups) Tomatoes, slices
(4 cups) Red bell peppers, slices
(6 cups) Chicken stock

COOKING STEPS:

1. Hit SOUP/STEW followed by TIME ADJUSTMENT and correct time to 15 minutes.

2. Heat the oil, sauté the onions, the garlic and the peppers until soft.

3. Add the tomatoes and the wine. Stir to combine

4. Add the potatoes and the stock. Stir to combine.

4. Place lid on cooker, lock the PRESSURE SEAL, and bring up to pressure.

5. Once done, release pressure by quick release method.

6. Transfer dish to a blender or food processor to get it completely smooth.

7. Bring it to bowl and serve it.

Mashed Sweet Potatoes

After 15 minutes cooking under high-pressure, you could mash those potatoes just by staring at them. The softness of the starch and the richness of the butter can make brothers fight for the last spoon. The cream joins the salt in the task of melting away our small-talks and bla-bla-blas, reminding us that the best dishes are the ones we eat in silence.

Serves: 4 - 6
Preparation Time: 7 minutes
Cooking Time: 15 minutes

INGREDIENTS:

Sugar, salt and pepper to taste
Butter to taste
(2 tbsp) Heavy cream

(1 cup) Water
(2 lbs) Sweet potatoes, peeled and sliced

COOKING STEPS:

1. Add potatoes, water and spices to the pot.

2. Hit SOUP/STEW followed by TIME ADJUSTMENT and correct time to 15 minutes.

3. Place lid on cooker, lock the PRESSURE SEAL, and bring up to pressure.

4. Once done, release pressure by quick release method.

5. Strain it and mash it.

7. Bring it to bowl and serve it with butter.

Pumpkin Apple Soup

This ambitious entree makes up for everlasting tedious dinners. The official getaway dish to vegetarianism, this soup is famous for summers and winters, as well as for lunches and dinners. It works great as a side dish but can easily take over the main meal glory with an optional portion of rice or bread.

Serves: 4 - 5
Preparation Time: 10 minutes
Cooking Time: 10 minutes

INGREDIENTS:

Butter to taste
Salt and pepper to taste
A pinch of curry powder
(2 tbsp) Bay leaves
(1 cup) Potatoes, diced

(1 cup) Onion, chopped
(1 cup) Apple, peeled, grated
(1 cup) Milk
(3 cups) Chicken stock
(4 cups) Butternut pumpkin, chunks

COOKING STEPS:

1. Hit SOUP/STEW followed by TIME ADJUSTMENT and correct time to 5 minutes.

2. Melt the butter, sauté the onions, the pumpkin, the potato until the onions are brown.

3. Add stock and bay leaves. Stir to combine.

3. Place lid on cooker, lock the PRESSURE SEAL, and bring up to pressure.

4. Once done, release pressure by quick release method.

5. Add the apples and let it cook for 5 minutes under the remaining heat. Stir to combine.

6. Remove the bay leaves and add the milk. Transfer soup to a blender or food processor to get it completely smooth.

7. Place the soup in a bowl and serve it.

Mushroom Barley Soup

This dish is a marathon of flavors. Each layer of seasoning brings a new aroma: the sherry, the mushroom, the garlic, the thyme. At the end, they meet at the barley. A simple but rich cereal that softens up easily under boiling broth, summing up every ingredient together like they've always belong in the same place. Enjoy it as a summer soup lunch or as an entree for meat or fish.

Serves: 4 - 5
Preparation Time: 10 minutes
Cooking Time: 15 minutes

INGREDIENTS:

Salt and pepper to taste
Butter to taste
(½ tbsp) Fresh thyme, chopped
(2 tbsp) Cloves garlic, smashed
(2 tbsp) Fresh parsley, chopped
(⅓ cup) Sherry

(¾ cup) Pearl barley
(1 cup) Onions, chopped
(1 cup) Cup carrots, peeled and diced
(5 cups) Chicken broth
(16 oz) Mushrooms, sliced

COOKING STEPS:

1. Hit SOUP/STEW followed by TIME ADJUSTMENT and correct time to 10 minutes.

2. Melt the butter, sauté the onions, the garlic and the carrots until brown.

3. Add the mushrooms and the thyme. Sauté until vegetables are soft.

4. Add sherry and cook until liquid evaporates.

5. Add barley and chicken broth. Stir to combine.

3. Place lid on cooker, lock the PRESSURE SEAL, and bring up to pressure.

4. Once done, release pressure by quick release method.

5. Remove bay leaves, add the parsley.

6. Place the soup in a bowl and serve it.

Italian White Bean Soup

This recipe reminds us that beans don't need to be black or red. Aim for the freshest ingredients and those little white marvels will become your family's new favorite bean. Here it cooks for over 60 minutes under high-pressure, way shorter than the 3 - 4 hours required by regular pots. Serve it with bread, olive oil and a top of fresh tard leaves.

Serves: 5 - 6
Preparation Time: 20 minutes
Cooking Time: 60 minutes

INGREDIENTS:

Olive oil to taste
Salt and pepper to taste
(1 tbsp) Rosemary, chopped
(2 tbsp) Thyme
(2 tbsp) Garlic, sliced
(½ cup) Sour cream
(1 cup) Onions, chopped

(2 cups) Carrots, chopped
(2 cups) Butternut squash, diced
(2 cups) Celery, chopped
(4 cups) Swiss chard leaves, chopped
(8 cups) Chicken stock
(16 oz) White beans, dry

COOKING STEPS:

1. Hit SOUP/STEW followed by TIME ADJUSTMENT and correct time to 35 minutes.

2. Heat the oil, sauté the onions, the garlic, the carrots and the celery until brown.

3. Add the beans, the herbs and the stock. Stir to combine.

4. Place lid on cooker, lock the PRESSURE SEAL, and bring up to pressure.

5. Once done, release pressure by quick release method.

6. Add in the squash and stir to combine.

7. Hit SOUP/STEW once again followed by TIME ADJUSTMENT and correct time to 10 minutes.

8. Place lid on cooker, lock the PRESSURE SEAL, and bring up to pressure.

9. Once done, release pressure by slow release method, letting the steam escape naturally.

10. Place soup in bowls, top with fresh chard leaves.

Minestrone

The classic soup entree. The nonna's signature dish. In Italy, every household is forced by law to prepare this dish once a week. That's not completely true, but it does feel like it. But with some sense: this soup is a rich and tasty collection of flavors that keeps its eaters warm for some good hours. After some experiments, replace the vegetables to your own taste and create your very own legume-broth soup. Serve it with pasta, cheese and whirl of olive oil.

Serves: 4 - 6
Preparation Time: 20 minutes
Cooking Time: 60 minutes

INGREDIENTS:

Salt and pepper to taste
Olive oil to taste
(2 tbsp) Fresh basil, chopped
(3 tbsp) Garlic, minced
(1 cup) Dry pasta, tortellini works great
(1 cup) Onions, chopped
(1 ½ cups) Carrots, diced
(1 cup) Celery, diced

(1 cup) Zucchini, chopped
(1 cup) Parmesan cheese, grated
(2 cups) Chicken broth
(2 cups) Baby spinach
(14 ½ oz) Canned kidney beans
(3 lbs) Tomatoes, peeled, seeded and chopped

COOKING STEPS:

1. Hit SOUP/STEW followed by TIME ADJUSTMENT and correct time to 5 minutes.

2. Heat the oil, sauté the vegetables (save the tomato and the spinach) until brown.

3. Add the tomatoes, the herbs and the stock. Salt to taste. Stir to combine.

4. Place lid on cooker, lock the PRESSURE SEAL, and bring up to pressure.

5. Once done, release pressure by quick release method.

6. Add in the spinach and stir to combine.

7. Bring soup to bowls, serve with topped parmesan cheese.

Cauliflower Mushroom Soup

The smart readers will notice this is a mixture of the broccoli cheese soup with the mushroom barley soup. The cooking process is similar, but the taste, hmm. The cauliflower fits so perfectly to the mushroom and the garlic, it can easily become a weekly family tradition. Serve with bread and fresh salad for a simple summer lunch.

Serves: 5 - 6
Preparation Time: 5 minutes
Cooking Time: 5 minutes

INGREDIENTS:

Salt and pepper to taste
Olive oil to taste
(2 tbsp) Thyme, dry
(2 tbsp) Garlic, chopped

(1 cup) Parmesan, grated
(4 cups) Mushrooms, sliced
(4 cups) Cauliflower, chopped
(6 cups) Vegetable stock

COOKING STEPS:

1. Hit BEANS/LENTILS followed by TIME ADJUSTMENT and correct time to 5 minutes.

2. Heat the oil and sauté the onion, the garlic and the mushrooms until brown. Season to taste.

3. Add remaining ingredients (save the parmesan for serving) and stir to combine.

4. Place lid on cooker, lock the PRESSURE SEAL, and bring up to pressure.

5. Once done, release pressure by slow release method, letting the steam escape naturally.

6. Bring dish to blender or food processor for creamy consistency. Top with parmesan and serve it along big chunks of bread and a swirl of olive oil.

Simple Spinach Soup

A great meal in 5 minutes, what else could you ask for? This soup is an amazing entree that will make everyone at home grow big smiles from ear to ear. Use frozen spinach or canned corn to save even more time and get straight to the interesting part: eating!

Serves: 4 - 5
Preparation Time: 5 minutes
Cooking Time: 5 minutes

INGREDIENTS:

Olive oil to taste.
Salt and pepper to taste.
(1 cup) Onions, diced
(1 cup) Carrots, diced

(2 cups) Corn, kernels, cooked
(5 cups) Vegetable stock
(4 oz) Bacon, strips
(10 oz) Spinach, chopped

COOKING STEPS:

1. Hit MEAT/CHICKEN followed by TIME ADJUSTMENT and correct time to 5 minutes.

2. Heat the oil and brown the onions and the bacon thoroughly.

3. Add corn, spinach and stock. Season to taste and stir to combine.

4. Place lid on cooker, lock the PRESSURE SEAL, and bring up to pressure.

5. Once done, release pressure by quick release method.

6. Transfer to bowls and serve.

Spinach Artichoke Dip

This brilliant recipe has been in the internet since the BBS times. Every grandma once shared a cut-out of this dip from a cookbook or magazine at some point in their lives. Not to wonder, as the artichoke has being part of our kitchen since 5 AD. Cultivated on the Mediterranean Eurasia and the North-African countries, the Italians took it to Florence where then the XIV chefs began experimenting with it. Now here it is, alive and well cooked under five minutes, ready for your afternoon snack time, brunch or midnight feast.

Serves: 5 - 6
Preparation Time: 5 minutes
Cooking Time: 5 minutes

INGREDIENTS:

Aluminum foil
Salt and pepper to taste
Olive oil to taste
(2 tbsp) Thyme, dry
(2 tbsp) Garlic, chopped
(½ cup) Sour cream

(1 cup) Parmesan, grated
(1 cup) Mayonnaise
(2 cups) Water for cooking
(14 oz) Artichoke, drained, rinsed, chopped
(10 oz) Spinach, frozen
(2 lbs) Baking dish, glass or ceramic

COOKING STEPS:

1. Mix every ingredient into the baking dish (without the water!). Cover tightly with aluminum foil.

2. Add STEAMER TRAY to the pot and pour in water. Place the dish over the tray.

3. Hit BEANS/LENTILS followed by TIME ADJUSTMENT and correct time to 10 minutes.

4. Place lid on cooker, lock the PRESSURE SEAL, and bring up to pressure.

5. Once done, release pressure by quick release method.

6. Carefully remove dish and serve it like a dip along bread and snacks.

Eggplant, Red Pepper and Olive Spread

This simple legume mingle transforms bread slices and sandwiches into meals. A classic member of the Italian antipasti, it has centuries of experience serving demanding palates next to cheese, fish and meat. Here, it saves you both time and work, cooking under high-pressure for only 20 minutes. Serve it as entree as well as a breakfast sandwich spread.

Serves: 3 - 4
Preparation Time: 10 minutes
Cooking Time: 20 minutes

INGREDIENTS:

Olive oil to taste
(1 tbsp) Thyme, chopped
(2 tbsp) Garlic, chopped
(1 cup) Onions, sliced
(1 cup) Black olives, seeded, pickled

(1 ½ cup) Vegetable stock
(2 cups) Red bell peppers, julienne
(2 cups) Carrots, julienne
(3 cups) Eggplant, julienne

COOKING STEPS:

1. Hit CANNING/PRESERVING followed by TIME ADJUSTMENT and correct time to 20 minutes.

2. Heat the oil in the pot. Add the onions, the garlic and the herbs. Sauté briefly.

3. Add the eggplant, the carrots and the peppers. Stir until brown.

4. Pour in the stock. Stir to combine.

5. Place lid on cooker, lock the PRESSURE SEAL, and bring up to pressure.

6. Once done, release pressure by slow release method, letting the steam escape naturally.

7. Transfer dish to jars and let it cool. Add olives and serve it as antipasti or morning bread spreads. Add olive oil if necessary. It lasts for 3 - 4 days in your fridge.

Hummus

This chickpea-tahini paste is an ancient secret from Arabian kitchens. There are records of this recipe in books since the 13th century. Today, all the chickpea needs is 20 minutes under high-pressure to become smooth and easy to handle. The tahini joins in and fixes it into a delicious nutty taste and form. Serve it in sandwiches, dips and entrees. Program yourself for the soaking of the chickpeas and let it happen over night. Add freshly squeezed lemons as served.

Serves: 3 - 4
Preparation Time: 10 minutes (plus 12 hours for soaking the chickpeas)
Cooking Time: 20 minutes

INGREDIENTS:

Olive oil to taste
Salt to taste
(¼ tbsp) Cumin, powder
(½ tbsp) Paprika, powder
(1 tbsp) Bay leaves
(2 tbsp) Garlic, chopped
(2 tbsp) Tahini

(¼ cup) Lemon, juiced
(¼ cup) Parsley, chopped
(1 cup) Onions, chopped
(1 cup) Dry chickpeas, soaked overnight in water
(6 cups) Water

PREPARATION:

1. In a bowl, add water and chickpeas, and let it soak for 12 hours.

COOKING STEPS:

1. Hit RICE/RISOTTO followed by TIME ADJUSTMENT and correct time to 18 minutes.

2. Heat the oil in the pot. Add the onions, the garlic, the herbs. Sauté briefly.

3. Add the chickpeas. Sauté briefly.

4. Pour in the water. Add the spices and season to taste. Stir to combine.

5. Place lid on cooker, lock the PRESSURE SEAL, and bring up to pressure.

6. Once done, release pressure by slow release method, letting the steam escape naturally.

7. Let it cool and strain chickpeas into a bowl. Save the liquid.

8. Transfer chickpeas to a blender or food processor. Add in the tahini, the lemon and blend until creamy paste thickness is reached. Adjust consistency with the saved chickpea water.

9. Bring hummus to jars and let it cool in the fridge. Serve as antipasti or bread spreads.

Boiled Peanuts

It's snack time! In this variation of the classic roasted treat, we introduce the soft and tasty peanut. A great appetizer to be made in bulk. Wash it well before cooking and watch out for the salt (it's easy to over or under salt it). Season it in layers as you remove skin and shells, and you are fine.

Serves: 5 - 6
Preparation Time: 5 minutes
Cooking Time: 25 minutes

INGREDIENTS:

Salt to taste
(4 cups) Water
(3 lbs) Peanuts, raw, rinsed

COOKING STEPS:

1. Add every ingredient to the pot and stir to combine.

2. Hit BEANS/LENTILS followed by TIME ADJUSTMENT and correct time to 25 minutes.

3. Place lid on cooker, lock the PRESSURE SEAL, and bring up to pressure.

4. Once done, release pressure by slow release method, letting the steam escape naturally.

5. Strain peanuts and remove shell and skin if desired. Season to adjust. Serve it cool or warm as a snack.

Potato Red Lentil Soup

Simple can be tasty. This soup brings such a variety of colors and aromas, and thanks to the easy cooking properties of the red lentil, you won't believe it can be done in 10 minutes. As always, try to use fresh curry leaves and fresh ginger and fresh everything. Double the recipe for a full meal or serve it as a side dish or entree.

Serves: 3 - 4
Preparation Time: 5 minutes
Cooking Time: 10 minutes

INGREDIENTS:

Vegetable oil to taste
Salt and pepper to taste
(1 tbsp) Ginger, ground
(1 tbsp) Curry, ground
(2 tbsp) Garlic, chopped
(1 cup) Onions, chopped

(1 cup) Red lentils, soaked
(1 cup) Cilantro, chopped
(1 ½ cups) Coconut milk
(2 cups) Vegetable stock
(1 lb) Potato, chunks

COOKING STEPS:

1. Hit MEAT/CHICKEN followed by TIME ADJUSTMENT and correct time to 10 minutes.

2. Heat the oil and sauté the garlic and the onions until brown.

3. Add the potatoes, the lentils, the stock, the curry and the ginger. Season to taste and stir to combine.

4. Place lid on cooker, lock the PRESSURE SEAL, and bring up to pressure.

5. Once done, release pressure by quick release method.

6. Add coconut milk and stir to combine. Bring dish to bowl, top with cilantro and serve.

Chole Masala

That's how you do your chickpeas in the Indian fashion. Use the ready-made spices blend or aim for the fresh turmeric and curry if you happen to live in Goa. It's a classic side dish for any other Indian food, pairing deliciously with a simple rice and salad for a full vegetarian meal.

Serves: 3 - 4
Preparation Time: 5 minutes (chickpeas need to be soaked overnight)
Cooking Time: 30 minutes

INGREDIENTS:

Vegetable oil to taste
Salt and pepper to taste
(½ tbsp) Cumin, ground
(½ tbsp) Coriander, ground
(½ tbsp) Turmeric, ground
(1 tbsp) Mustard
(1 tbsp) Curry, ground

(2 tbsp) Garlic, chopped
(1 cup) Onions, chopped
(1 cup) Chickpeas, soaked overnight
(1 cup) Potato, chunks
(1 cup) Tomato, diced and cored
(1 cup) Cilantro, chopped
(2 cups) Vegetable stock

COOKING STEPS:

1. Hit SOUP/LENTILS followed by TIME ADJUSTMENT and correct time to 30 minutes.

2. Heat the oil and sauté the garlic and the onions until brown.

3. Add the tomatoes, the potatoes, the chickpeas, the stock and the spices. Season to taste and stir to combine.

4. Place lid on cooker, lock the PRESSURE SEAL, and bring up to pressure.

5. Once done, release pressure by slow release method, letting the steam escape naturally.

6. Bring dish to bowl, top with cilantro and serve as a side dish with rice and salad.

Summer Beans

This bean recipe works great as a warm side dish and also as a cold salad. With some extra vegetable stock, it can become a delicious soup. Serve it with rice and bring it in for a pleasant surprise in that family's barbecue or friend's potluck.

Serves: 4 - 5
Preparation Time: 5 minutes (beans need to be soaked overnight)
Cooking Time: 25 minutes

INGREDIENTS:

Vegetable oil to taste
Salt and pepper to taste
(2 tbsp) Garlic, chopped
(½ cup) Lemon, juice
(½ cup) Cilantro, chopped
(1 cup) Onions, chopped

(1 cup) Tomato, diced and cored
(3 cups) Vegetable stock
(2 ½ cups) Beans (white and pinto are great), soaked overnight
(3 cups) Spinach, chopped

COOKING STEPS:

1. Hit SOUP/LENTILS followed by TIME ADJUSTMENT and correct time to 25 minutes.

2. Heat the oil and sauté the garlic and the onions until brown.

3. Add the beans, the tomatoes, and the stock. Season to taste and stir to combine.

4. Place lid on cooker, lock the PRESSURE SEAL, and bring up to pressure.

5. Once done, release pressure by quick release method.

6. Add lemon juice and spinach. Season to adjust. Stir to combine and let the remaining heat cook the spinach for 3 to 5 minutes.

7. Bring dish to bowl, top with cilantro and serve as a side. Let it cool down and serve like a salad.

Refried Beans

That's what we Brazilians call Tutu. It's basically a mashed bean dish. This Latin recipe is very simple and yet tasty. And you can always pimp it up with bacon or any other ingredient. Mexicans serve it with a top of cilantro and cheese, but we Brazilians like it with kale and pork. Serve it in your own style and make history!

Serves: 4 - 5
Preparation Time: 5 minutes (beans need to be soaked overnight)
Cooking Time: 25 minutes

INGREDIENTS:

Vegetable oil to taste
Salt and pepper to taste
(2 tbsp) Garlic, chopped
(½ cup) Cilantro, chopped

(1 cup) Onions, chopped
(3 cups) Vegetable stock
(2 ½ cups) Beans (black and pinto are great), soaked overnight

COOKING STEPS:

1. Hit SOUP/LENTILS followed by TIME ADJUSTMENT and correct time to 25 minutes.

2. Heat the oil and sauté the garlic and the onions until brown.

3. Add the beans, and the stock. Season to taste and stir to combine.

4. Place lid on cooker, lock the PRESSURE SEAL, and bring up to pressure.

5. Once done, release pressure by quick release method.

6. Bring dish to blender or food processor for creamy consistency.

7. Bring dish to bowl, top with cilantro and cheese, or serve as a side dish with kale and rice.

BREAKFAST

Creamy Scrambled Eggs

Now you can make breakfast easily under high-pressure. Stir and mix the eggs with the cheese for a delicious scrambled egg. So easy, so simple, we will let your imagination run wild and fill in the gaps here. Serve it as breakfast with toast and butter.

Serves: 4
Preparation Time: 5 minutes
Cooking Time: 5 minutes

INGREDIENTS:

Vegetable oil to taste
(1 tbsp) Thyme, chopped
(1 cup) Spring onions, chopped

(1 cup) Cream
(1 cup) Cheese, mozzarella
(3 cups) 8 eggs, beaten

PREPARATION:

1. In a bowl, mix the beaten eggs with the cream and reserve.

COOKING STEPS:

1. Hit FISH/VEG/STEAM followed by TIME ADJUSTMENT and correct time to 4 minutes.

2. Heat the oil in the pot. Add the spring onion and the herbs. Sauté briefly.

3. Pour the egg mixture in the pot. Stir to combine.

4. Place lid on cooker, lock the PRESSURE SEAL, and bring up to pressure.

6. Once done, release pressure by quick release method.

7. Add cheese. Stir to combine. Bring eggs to plates and serve with toast and butter.

Omelet

Let's be very honest here, this is a simple variation of the scrambled egg. Let the egg mixture sink in smoothly through the legumes and you get a fancy omelet. Vary the ingredients until you find the perfect quick lunch for you family. Serve it as breakfast as well as lunch or supper.

Serves: 4
Preparation Time: 5 minutes
Cooking Time: 5 minutes

INGREDIENTS:

Vegetable oil to taste
(1 tbsp) Garlic, chopped
(1 tbsp) Thyme, chopped
(1 cup) Spring onions, chopped

(1 cup) Cream
(2 cups) Zucchinis, sliced
(2 cups) Carrots, sliced
(3 cups) 8 eggs, beaten

PREPARATION:

1. In a bowl, mix the beaten eggs with the cream and reserve.

COOKING STEPS:

1. Hit FISH/VEG/STEAM followed by TIME ADJUSTMENT and correct time to 4 minutes.

2. Heat the oil in the pot. Add the spring onion, the garlic and the herbs. Sauté briefly.

3. Add the zucchinis and the carrots. Sauté until brown. Season to taste.

4. Pour the egg mixture in the pot. Stir for scrambled, let it sink in for omelet.

5. Place lid on cooker, lock the PRESSURE SEAL, and bring up to pressure.

6. Once done, release pressure by quick release method.

7. Cut omelet in pies and serve with toast and butter for breakfast or with salad for lunch or dinner.

Sausage Hash Brown

Also known as the farmer's breakfast, this dish serves well the young, the old, the fancy and the simple. Break a few beaten eggs on top to make it an extraordinary casserole for lunch. Serve it as a side or main dish with a spoon of dark gravy.

Serves: 4 - 6
Preparation Time: 10 minutes
Cooking Time: 15 minutes

INGREDIENTS:

Olive oil to taste.

Salt and pepper to taste.

(1 ½ cup) Onions, diced

(1 ½ cup) Vegetable stock

(1 lb) Italian sausage, ground

(2 lbs) Potatoes, thin sliced

COOKING STEPS:

1. Hit MEAT/CHICKEN followed by TIME ADJUSTMENT and correct time to 15 minutes.

2. Heat the oil and brown the onions and the sausage thoroughly. Season to taste. Once brown and well-done, remove everything to a bowl and reserve.

3. Add potatoes and stock to the pot. Stir to combine.

4. Place lid on cooker, lock the PRESSURE SEAL, and bring up to pressure.

5. Once done, release pressure by quick release method.

6. Bring sausage to the pot and stir to combine. Transfer to bowls and serve.

Eggs En Cocotte

As the delicious egg and cheese mixture stands in front of you, begging to be eaten, the hot bowl teaches you the noble art of patience. In reality, this is a recipe for discipline. Let it cool, my friend. Let this morning delight wait a few minutes and enjoy it without risk.

Serves: 4
Preparation Time: 5 minutes
Cooking Time: 8 minutes

INGREDIENTS:

Olive oil to taste
Salt and pepper to taste
Herbs to taste (thyme and oregano work great)
(8 tbsp) Cream

(4 tbsp) Cheese, (parmesan works amazingly), grated
(8 oz) Glass or ceramic bowl
(4 cups) Water
(24 oz) 12 eggs

PREPARATION:

1. Break 3 eggs in each bowl.

2. Add 2 tbsp of cream and 1 tbsp of cheese on top of each bowl and season with herbs. Season to taste.

COOKING STEPS:

1. Add STEAMER TRAY and pour in water. Place the bowls and make sure they are halfway covered with water.

2. Hit FISH/VEGETABLES/STEAM followed by TIME ADJUSTMENT and correct time to 8 minutes.

3. Place lid on cooker, lock the PRESSURE SEAL, and bring up to pressure.

4. Once done, release pressure by quick release method.

5. Carefully remove bowls and place them over plates. Serve and alert everyone about the heat!

High Pressure Boiled Eggs

If you need to boil a bunch of eggs in bulk, that's your best option. You can cook from 12 to 15 eggs in this machine. Try it out for yourself and get your morning going strong with those delicious, healthy and simple treats. Cut cooking time in half for soft boiled eggs. Add salt and pepper and that's all.

Serves: 4 - 5
Preparation Time: 15 minutes
Cooking Time: 30 minutes (plus a few hours cooling in the fridge)

INGREDIENTS:

(4 cups) Water for cooking

(4 cups) 12 eggs

COOKING STEPS:

1. Add STEAMER TRAY and pour in water. Place eggs over the tray.

2. Hit FISH/VEG/STEAM followed by TIME ADJUSTMENT and correct time to 6 minutes.

3. Place lid on cooker, lock the PRESSURE SEAL, and bring up to pressure.

4. Once done, release pressure by quick release method.

5. Carefully remove eggs. Let it cool briefly and serve cake along biscuits, snacks and refreshments.

Lemon Quinoa

The morning cereal from the Incas, today broadly spread throughout every corner of the world. Cook it with salt and make it a great topping for salads. Cook it with sugar and enjoy it with fruits. Serve it for lunch or breakfast with a dash of fresh lemon juice, cream or yogurt.

Serves: 4 - 5
Preparation Time: 5 minutes
Cooking Time: 15 minutes

INGREDIENTS:

Olive oil to taste
Salt and pepper to taste
(2 tbsp) Thyme, dry

(½ cup) 1 lemon, juiced
(3 cups) Water/vegetable stock
(2 cups) Quinoa, whole, quickly rinsed

COOKING STEPS:

1. Hit FISH/VEGETABLES/STEAM followed by TIME ADJUSTMENT and correct time to 15 minutes.

2. Heat the oil, add the quinoa and the herbs. Season to taste. Sauté quinoa briefly until grains start to pop. Add in the stock/water and stir to combine.

3. Place lid on cooker, lock the PRESSURE SEAL, and bring up to pressure.

4. Once done, release pressure by quick release method.

5. Add the lemon and stir to combine. Serve the hot or cold quinoa along salads and steamed vegetables. Avoid salt and you can serve it with fruit salad and yogurt.

Egg Carrot Muffins

There's always a different way of cooking eggs. Here, they merge with the carrots and the cheese, creating a delicate layer of deliciousness that cooks perfectly fast under high-pressure. Keep it healthy and serve it along fresh fruit juice, or grease it up with fried bacon while mom is not looking.

Serves: 4
Preparation Time: 5 minutes
Cooking Time: 8 minutes

INGREDIENTS:

Olive oil to taste
Salt and pepper to taste
(2 tbsp) Oregano
(½ cup) Onions, diced
(1 cup) Carrots, grated

(4 tbsp) Cheese, (parmesan works amazingly), grated
(8 oz) Baking dish, glass or ceramic
(4 cups) Water
(24 oz) 12 eggs

PREPARATION:

1. In a large mixing bowl, beat the eggs as you add every ingredient (besides water).

2. Stir to combine and season to taste.

3. Bring the egg mixture to each 8 oz bowl evenly.

COOKING STEPS:

1. Add STEAMER TRAY and pour in water. Place the bowls in and make sure they are halfway covered with water.

2. Hit FISH/VEGETABLES/STEAM followed by TIME ADJUSTMENT and correct time to 8 minutes.

3. Place lid on cooker, lock the PRESSURE SEAL, and bring up to pressure.

4. Once done, release pressure by quick release method.

5. Carefully remove bowls and place them over plates. Serve and alert everyone about the heat!

Apple Oatmeal

Simple shouldn't be boring. Here we prove that even oatmeal can be pimped up and become a delight. Cook it for simple 5 minutes under high-pressure to transform a tasteless dry cereal into a fancy porridge. Add fruits to your own taste, experiment with different fruit juices and make this recipe uniquely yours.

Serves: 4 - 5
Preparation Time: 5 minutes
Cooking Time: 5 minutes

INGREDIENTS:

Salt and sugar to taste
(1 tbsp) Ginger, grated
(2 cups) Apples, diced

(2 ½ cups) Water/fruit juice
(2 cups) Oatmeal, whole

COOKING STEPS:

1. Add the apples, the oatmeal, the ginger and season to taste. Add the water and stir to combine.

2. Hit FISH/VEGETABLES/STEAM followed by TIME ADJUSTMENT and correct time to 5 minutes.

3. Place lid on cooker, lock the PRESSURE SEAL, and bring up to pressure.

4. Once done, release pressure by quick release method.

5. Stir to combine. Serve it hot or cold along fruit salad, fruit jam or yogurt.

Bread

A bread cooked in high-pressure? Well, bread is a broad word. You might better call it a wet loaf or a cake-like-bread. This moist and succulent side dish works great for emergencies and family surprises. Cut it in slices and toast it for the classic crispy bread texture.

Serves: 4 - 5
Preparation Time: 40 minutes
Cooking Time: 20 minutes

INGREDIENTS:

Salt to taste
(3 cups) Water for dough
(4 cups) Bread mix flour, wheat is fine

(2 lbs) Baking dish, glass or ceramic
(4 cups) Water for cooking

PREPARATION:

1. In a bowl, mix the flour and the water until it forms a firm dough. Kneel if necessary.

2. Let the mixture rest in room temperature for 30 minutes to 12 hours.

COOKING STEPS:

1. Bring the bread dough into the baking dish.

2. Add STEAMER TRAY and pour in water. Place the dish over the tray.

3. Hit CANNING/PRESERVING followed by TIME ADJUSTMENT and correct time to 20 minutes.

4. Place lid on cooker, lock the PRESSURE SEAL, and bring up to pressure.

5. Once done, release pressure by quick release method.

6. Carefully remove bowl. Let it cool briefly and carefully remove the bread. Cut in slices and serve it along butter or, well, almost anything.

Cheese Grits

The Native-American version of polenta, this dish takes a different form and taste in the new world. Here we update it with cheese and bring it to life in fast and simple recipe. Eat it for lunch, breakfast or supper. Mix it with steamed vegetables and you get a great meal coming along.

Serves: 4 - 5
Preparation Time: 5 minutes
Cooking Time: 15 minutes

INGREDIENTS:

Salt to taste
(2 tbsp) Butter, melted
(4 cups) Water for dough
(2 cups) Cornflour, whole

(1 cup) Cheese, parmesan work fine, grated
(4 cups) Water for cooking
(2 lbs) Baking dish, glass or ceramic

COOKING STEPS:

1. In the baking dish, mix the cornflour, the butter, the water and the salt to combine.

2. Add STEAMER TRAY and pour in water. Place the baking dish over the tray.

3. Hit CANNING/PRESERVING followed by TIME ADJUSTMENT and correct time to 15 minutes.

4. Place lid on cooker, lock the PRESSURE SEAL, and bring up to pressure.

5. Once done, release pressure by quick release method.

6. Carefully remove bowl. Top with cheese and serve for breakfast with eggs or for lunch along steamed vegetables and meat.

Fruit Jam-Marmalade

Here the possibilities are endless. Learn the different ratios of sugar X water/juice for each fruit and adapt it to your own taste. The heat and the pressure will reduce the fruit to a healthy and delicious bread spread. Choose fresh fruits that are currently abundant in your city and season (that's how you get better offers for bulk). Jams can get very bitter with certain types of skins, watch out for oranges and dark grapes and peel them off. Mix in different juices and spices to add layers of flavor. Serve it over cereals, fresh fruits or bread, biscuits and cakes.

Serves: 3 - 4
Preparation Time: 5 minutes
Cooking Time: 8 minutes

INGREDIENTS:

(½ cup) Unsalted butter
(1 cup) Fresh fruit (orange, grape and apple work great), juiced

(2 cups) Sugar
(2 lbs) Any citrus fruit (orange, apples, pears and strawberries work great) diced, cored

COOKING STEPS:

1. Hit FISH/VEG/STEAM followed by TIME ADJUSTMENT and correct time to 8 minutes.

2. Melt the butter and bring in the sugar. Stir constantly until caramelized.

3. Add the diced fruit. Stir briefly until brown.

4. Pour in the juice. Stir to combine.

5. Place lid on cooker, lock the PRESSURE SEAL, and bring up to pressure.

6. Once done, release pressure by slow release method, letting the steam escape naturally.

7. Let the jam cool and transfer to jars. Keep in the fridge for up 6 to 7 days or do some serious canning with it for a longer shelf life. Serve it as morning bread spread or as granola and fruit salad topping.

DESSERTS

Apple Cheesecake

In this hack we teach you how to bake a whole cake in high-pressure. The ricotta and the egg form the perfect base for the apples that, well, you have to taste to believe. Once cool and chilled, this wet cake begs to become a family tradition.

Serves: 4 - 5
Preparation Time: 15 minutes
Cooking Time: 20 minutes (plus a few hours cooling in the fridge)

INGREDIENTS:

Vegetable oil to grease dish
(1 tbsp) Vanilla
(2 tbsp) Egg
(2 tbsp) Baking powder
(1 cup) Sugar

(1 cup) Flour, wheat or corn
(1 cup) Cheese, ricotta
(4 cups) Water for cooking
(4 cups) Apples, grated and sliced
(2 lbs) Baking dish, glass or ceramic

PREPARATION:

1. In a mixing bowl, add the egg, the ricotta, the sugar, the flour, the vanilla and the diced apples. Stir to combine. Reserve.

2. Grease the baking dish with oil and cover the bottom with sliced apples. Pour the egg/ricotta mixture over the apples.

COOKING STEPS:

1. Add STEAMER TRAY and pour in water. Place the baking dish over the tray.

2. Hit CANNING/PRESERVING followed by TIME ADJUSTMENT and correct time to 20 minutes.

3. Place lid on cooker, lock the PRESSURE SEAL, and bring up to pressure.

4. Once done, release pressure by slow release method, letting the steam escape naturally.

5. Carefully remove dish. Let it cool briefly and carefully remove the cake. Let it cool down in the fridge. Cut in slices and top it with cream. Serve the cake along biscuits, snacks and refreshments.

Carrot Cake

Another cake hack for your high-pressure machine. This time the eggs meet the flour for a simple but creamy treat. This delicious cake becomes a wonder with chocolate and cream. And it keeps everyone happy and alert for the last piece once served along tea or coffee.

Serves: 4 - 5
Preparation Time: 15 minutes
Cooking Time: 30 minutes

INGREDIENTS:

Salt to taste
(1 cup) Vegetable oil
(2 tbsp) Baking powder
(2 cups) 6 eggs
(3 cups) Water for dough

(4 cups) Flour, wheat/corn
(4 cups) Sugar
(4 cups) Water for cooking
(4 cups) Carrots, grated
(2 lbs) Baking dish, glass or ceramic

COOKING STEPS:

1. In a mixing bowl, stir every ingredient until a lumpy dough. Pour cake dough into baking dish.

2. Add STEAMER TRAY and pour in water. Place the baking dish over the tray.

3. Hit CANNING/PRESERVING followed by TIME ADJUSTMENT and correct time to 30 minutes.

4. Place lid on cooker, lock the PRESSURE SEAL, and bring up to pressure.

5. Once done, release pressure by quick release method.

6. Carefully remove dish. Let it cool briefly and carefully remove the cake. Cut in slices and top it with chocolate and nuts. Serve the cake along biscuits, snacks and refreshments.

Flan

Also known ascaramel, this fancy dish asks for a selfie. Here we bring a recipe for individual portions with the perfect mixture of sugar, egg and milk. Such a simple and delicious idea, the cook who invented this dessert deserves our toast.

Serves: 4
Preparation Time: 15 minutes
Cooking Time: 15 minutes (plus a few hours cooling in the fridge)

INGREDIENTS:

Aluminium foil
(1 tbsp) 1 egg yolk
(1 tbsp) Vanilla
(2 cups) 5 eggs, whole
(¾ cup for flan) Sugar

(1 cup for caramel) Sugar
(6 oz each) 4 baking bowls, glass or ceramic
(4 cups) Water for cooking
(2 cups) Milk

PREPARATION:

1. In a regular stove pot, add the milk, the vanilla and heat to almost boiling point. Remove from heat, let it cool and reserve.

2. In a regular stove pot, add the sugar (for caramel) and heat until caramelized.

3. Whisk the eggs, the yolk and the sugar (for flan). Pour eggs into milk and stir to combine.

4. Pour the caramel into the baking bowls evenly.

5. Pour the milk/egg mixture into the baking bowls. Cover bowls tightly with aluminium foil.

COOKING STEPS:

1. Add STEAMER TRAY and pour in water. Place the bowls over the tray. Make sure they are halfway covered with water.

3. Hit FISH/VEG/STEAM followed by TIME ADJUSTMENT and correct time to 15 minutes.

4. Place lid on cooker, lock the PRESSURE SEAL, and bring up to pressure.

5. Once done, release pressure by quick release method.

6. Carefully remove bowls. Let it cool and bring it to the fridge. Once cold, place bowls upside down over dessert plates until the flan pops out and serve.

Crème Brûlée

The cousin of the flan, this dessert makes French cuisine look amazingly sophisticated. This simple egg, vanilla, cream deliciousness is the perfect end for any meal. Torch the sugar at the top for an extraordinary visual effect and let everyone wonder where you got your caramelizing skills.

Serves: 4
Preparation Time: 15 minutes
Cooking Time: 30 minutes

INGREDIENTS:

Aluminium foil
(1 tbsp) Vanilla
(3 tbsp) 6 eggs yolk
(⅓ cup) Sugar

(8 oz each) 4 baking bowls, glass or ceramic
(1 ½ cup) Cream
(4 cups) Water for cooking

PREPARATION:

1. In a large mixing bowl, whisk the eggs, the sugar, the cream and the vanilla until combined. Pour mixture into baking bowls and cover tightly with aluminum foil.

COOKING STEPS:

1. Add STEAMER TRAY and pour in water. Place the baking bowls over the tray. Make sure they are halfway covered with water.

2. Hit FISH/VEG/STEAM followed by TIME ADJUSTMENT and correct time to 8 minutes.

3. Place lid on cooker, lock the PRESSURE SEAL, and bring up to pressure.

4. Once done, release pressure by slow release method, letting the steam escape naturally.

5. Carefully remove bowls. Let it cool and bring it to the fridge. Once cold, serve with a top of freshly torched caramel.

Lemon Ricotta Cheesecake

Cooked directly in the glass jar, this dessert lures the mouth as well as the eyes. But be prepared: it asks for a bit of kitchen work and skill. Dive a bit more into baking techniques and this will be like frying an egg for a chef. Wait for it to cool and serve it right from the jar. And note, those portions are big. You can fix it by serving it like a sharing pot kind of meal (like popcorn). Give each person a spoon and watch them gladiate for the deliciousness of the sweet lemon and cheese.

Serves: 4
Preparation Time: 15 minutes
Cooking Time: 20 minutes (plus 5 hours cooling)

INGREDIENTS:

Aluminium foil
(2 tbsp) Unsalted Butter
(2 tbsp) Lemon zest, grated
(¼ cup) Lemon juice
(⅓ cup) Sugar
(1 tbsp) Vanilla, dry or extract
(½ cup) 2 eggs, beaten

(1 cup) Chocolate, grated
(4 oz) Plain cookies, or any other flour based sweet biscuit
(6 oz) Ricotta cheese, drained
(8 oz) Cream cheese
(16 oz each) 4 glass jars

PREPARATION:

1. In a blender or food processor, blend the cookies and set aside.

COOKING STEPS:

1. Hit CANNING/PRESERVING, add the butter to the pot, cook until melting. Hit CANCEL.

2. Add the butter to the cookies and blend again until a paste is formed.

3. In each 16oz jar, add a layer of the cookie paste to the bottom, no deeper than a quarter of an inch. Set the jars aside in the fridge for cooling.

4. In a bowl, mix the cheeses, breaking the ricotta with a fork. Add the sugar, the lemon and the vanilla gradually. Once well mixed, add in the beaten eggs. Mix and beat the mixture until pancake batter texture.

6. Bring the jars out. Pour the cheese mixture in, over the cookie dough. Cover jars tightly with aluminium foil.

7. Wipe the butter clean from the pot and add in the STEAMER TRAY. Cover ¼ of the pot with water. Add the jars.

8. Hit CANNING/PRESERVING followed by TIME ADJUSTMENT and correct time to 20 minutes.

9. Place lid on cooker, lock the PRESSURE SEAL, and bring up to pressure.

10. Once done, release pressure by slow release method, letting the steam escape naturally.

11. Remove the jars carefully and let them cool for about 1 hour.

12. Remove aluminium foil, lock the jars with lid and let them cool in the fridge for 4 hours.

13. Top the cheesecake with the chocolate and serve it directly in the jar.

Blueberry Cake

Yet another amazing cake variation for your pressure cooker. This time the blueberry joins the vanilla, the apple juice and the flour in an appetizing and sugar-free cake. Keep track of the pressure and the time to master the art of high-pressure cooking-baking. Serve it with cream for a delicious dessert or plain and dry along tea and biscuits.

Serves: 4 - 5
Preparation Time: 15 minutes
Cooking Time: 30 minutes (plus a few hours cooling in the fridge)

INGREDIENTS:

Aluminium foil
Vegetable oil to grease dish
(1 tbsp) Vanilla
(2 tbsp) Baking powder
(1 cup) Flour, wheat or corn

(½ cup) Apple juice
(2 cups) Blueberries
(4 cups) Water for cooking
(2 lbs) Baking dish, glass or ceramic

PREPARATION:

1. In a mixing bowl, add every ingredient and stir until a lumpy dough. Reserve.

2. Grease the baking dish with oil. Pour the cake mixture over and cover tightly with aluminium foil.

COOKING STEPS:

1. Add STEAMER TRAY and pour in water. Place the dish over the tray.

2. Hit CANNING/PRESERVING followed by TIME ADJUSTMENT and correct time to 30 minutes.

3. Place lid on cooker, lock the PRESSURE SEAL, and bring up to pressure.

4. Once done, release pressure by slow release method, letting the steam escape naturally.

5. Carefully remove dish. Let it cool briefly and carefully remove the cake. Let it cool down in the fridge. Cut in slices and serve the cake along biscuits, snacks and refreshments.

Ultimate Chocolate Fruit Salad

This is a fondue recipe converted into a sauce for desserts. Done fast and easy under high pressure, it goes perfectly well with apples, bananas, pineapples, pears, oranges, mangoes, strawberries, raspberries, blueberries and, well every type of berry and fruit. Experiment with the possibilities and discover what works for you and your family.

Serves: 4
Preparation Time: 15 minutes
Cooking Time: 20 minutes (plus 1 hour cooling)

INGREDIENTS:

Aluminium foil
(4 tbsp) Fruit liqueur
(2 cups) Fresh cream
(1 cup) Chocolate, grated

(2 cups) Chocolate, chunks
(4 cups) Fruit salad
(16 oz) 4 glass jars

COOKING STEPS:

1. Add ½ a cup of chocolate and ½ cup of fresh cream to each jar. Add liqueur if desired. Seal the jars tightly with the aluminum foil.

2. Insert the STEAMER TRAY into the pot. Cover ¼ of the pot with water. Add the jars.

3. Hit FISH/VEG/STEAM and set time to default (2 minutes).

4. Place lid on cooker, lock the PRESSURE SEAL, and bring up to pressure.

5. Once done, release pressure by slow release method, letting the steam escape naturally.

6. Remove the jars carefully and let them cool completely.

7. Remove aluminium foil, add in the fruits.

8. Top the fruits with the grated chocolate and serve directly in the jar.

Apple Cinnamon Ginger Sauce

The beauty of this sauce is that you can choose to have the fruit in pieces, or in a paste. Both are great in taste and texture. Use the pieces with fresh fruits and cereals for breakfast. The paste serves a ingredient for cakes, candies, biscuits. Mix them together and you get a delicious jam for breakfast and snacks.

Serves: 4
Preparation Time: 10 minutes
Cooking Time: 5 minutes (plus cooling time)

INGREDIENTS:

(1 tbsp) Cinnamon, ground
(4 tbsp) Ginger, grated
(¼ cup) Sugar

(½ cup) Apple juice
(1 cup) Chocolate, grated
(10 cups) Apples, peeled, cored, quartered

COOKING STEPS:

1. Add all the ingredient into the pot. Stir to combine.

2. Hit BEANS/LENTILS and set time to default (5 minutes).

3. Place lid on cooker, lock the PRESSURE SEAL, and bring up to pressure.

4. Once done, release pressure by quick release method.

5. Stir to combine. Bring apple sauce to jars for cooling. (You can also liquify it in a blender or food processor for a creamy consistency - perfect for layering candies and cakes).

6. Serve the dessert in bowls with a top of ginger.

Banana Rice Pudding

From a simple evening dessert to a rich morning breakfast meal. It works with any rice, really, but stick to the milky and starchy ones for the pudding consistency. Experiment by serving it with different fruits accordingly to season or location. Add cinnamon for desserts and serve it with a shot of espresso.

Serves: 4
Preparation Time: 15 minutes
Cooking Time: 20 minutes (plus 1 hour cooling)

INGREDIENTS:

A pinch cinnamon (optional)
(½ tbsp) Vanilla
(½ cup) 2 eggs, beaten
(½ cup) Sugar

(1 cup) Rice
(1 ½ cup) Water
(2 cups) Milk
(2 cups) Bananas, sliced

COOKING STEPS:

1. Add the rice, the water and salt into the pot. Stir to combine.

3. Hit BEANS/LENTILS and set time to default (5 minutes).

4. Place lid on cooker, lock the PRESSURE SEAL, and bring up to pressure.

5. Once done, release pressure by slow release method, letting the steam escape naturally.

6. In a bowl, mix the eggs, the sugar and the vanilla. Whisk to blend.

7. Add in the egg mix into the pot. Stir to combine.

8. Hit BEANS/LENTILS once again. Sauté the rice, stirring constantly until creamy consistency. Once done, hit CANCEL.

9. Pour the rice into bowls. Add the bananas for that healthy breakfast feeling. Serve with a pinch of cinnamon.

Dulce de Leche

This is the ultimate stovetop hack, here converted to the 2016 home appliance regulations of safety and common-sense. It works deliciously as a paste with almonds or every other nut. And it goes really well with anything that needs sweetness, like citrus fruits, breads or biscuits. But remember: balance the dulce de leche well with the healthy fresh food and don't overdose on this thing!

Serves: 10-16
Preparation Time: 15 minutes
Cooking Time: 20 minutes (plus 1 hour cooling)

INGREDIENTS:

Aluminium foil
(16 oz each) 4 clean glass jars
(56 oz) 4 cans sweetened condensed milk
(8 cups) Water

COOKING STEPS:

1. Pour condensed milk into jars and cover tightly with aluminium foil.

2. Put steamer rack into pot. Pour the water in and place the jars in the pot.

3- Hit CANNING/PRESERVING and set time to 30 minutes.

4. Place lid on cooker, lock the PRESSURE SEAL, and bring up to pressure.

5. Once done, release pressure by quick release method.

6- Remove jars carefully and let them cool off completely.

6. Serve dulce de leche as a bread spread, or save it for filling cakes and candies.

Yogurt

The closed ambient from the machine provides the perfect place for the milk cultures to develop. Here, we hacked your machine and teach you how to create this delicious sauce that mixes in perfectly with salads, fruits, cereals, cakes and biscuits. Experiment with different yogurt types and milks to develop your own cultures. Watch out for the difference between sour and foul in both taste and aroma. It should not be repulsive, but enticing. Mix in sugar and fruit jam to hack the typical supermarket industrialized recipe.

Serves: 4 - 6
Preparation Time: 10 minutes
Cooking Time: 30 minutes

INGREDIENTS:

Aluminium foil
(½ cup) Yoghurt, whole
(2 cups) Water

(8 cups) Milk, whole
(16 oz each) 4 clean glass jars

COOKING STEPS:

1. Pour the milk in the jars evenly.

2. Place STEAM RACK in the pot and add 2 cups of water. Place jars over the rack.

3. Hit FISH/VEG/STEAM and set time to default (2 minutes).

4. Wait for milk to scald. Watch out for the point before the milk is about to boil. Press CANCEL and turn the machine completely off.

5. Remove the jars. Wait for them to be cool enough to handle.

6. Add the yoghurt in the jars (around 2 tablespoons each). Whisk gently to combine. Seal tightly with aluminium foil.

7. Place jars back in the pot. Place lid on cooker. Make sure the machine is completely off. Look for lukewarm temperatures. Anything over 110F will prevent the yogurt from reproducing.

8. After 6 to 12 hours, check in for milk coagulation. Look for firm, sour and tasty bits.

9. Transfer jars to fridge and keep them up to 6 or 7 days. Use it as a base for salad sauces, or with fruit jam, cereal and pancakes. You can reuse the culture and make more joghurt.

BROTHS, STOCKS AND SAUCES

Fish Stock

When dealing with those parts of fish you have to know your sources. Talk to your fisherman, or that helpful lady in the supermarket. Pay extra attention to the frozen fish and be well versed in the art of butchering spines. Learn to spot the rotting bits and wash and rinse every bone carefully before summoning this delicious sauce of the sea. Use it often with Asian recipes and don't be afraid of heating it up with spices.

Serves: 5 cups
Preparation Time: 15 minutes
Cooking Time: 30 minutes

INGREDIENTS:

Salt and pepper to taste
(1 tbsp) Garlic, whole
(2 tbsp) Parsley, chopped
(1 tbsp) Bay leaf
(1 cup) Onions, chunks
(1 cup) Celery, chunks

(1 cup) Dry white wine
(2 cups) Carrots, chunks
(4 cups) Water
(1 lbs) Any whitefish, whole, include bones and head, rinsed, chunks

COOKING STEPS:

1. Combine all the ingredients in the pot.

2. Hit CANNING/PRESERVING and set time to 30 minutes.

3. Place lid on cooker, lock the PRESSURE SEAL, and bring up to pressure.

4. Once done, release pressure by quick release method.

5. Strain the liquid and discard the solids. Let it cool and place the stock in jars for future use. It lasts 3 - 4 days in the fridge.

Vegetable Stock

You have to learn this recipe before even learning how to make rice. In this version, we take it through the high-pressure, reducing to 40 minutes what used to take over 2 hours. Remember to always taste and correct the seasoning. And, depending on the freshness of the ingredients you use, the discard could be gold. Save it for filling veggie burgers or reduce it even further to a paste for a great natural thickening agent for sauces.

Serves: 5 cups
Preparation Time: 10 minutes
Cooking Time: 30 minutes

INGREDIENTS:

Vegetable oil to taste
Salt and pepper to taste
(1 tbsp) Bay leaf
(2 tbsp) Garlic
(2 tbsp) Thyme

(1 cup) Onion, chunks
(1 cup) Tomatoes, quartered
(2 cups) Carrots, chunks
(2 cups) Celery, chopped
(5 cups) Water

COOKING STEPS:

1. Hit CANNING/PRESERVING and set time to 30 minutes.

2. Heat the oil in the pot. Add all the vegetables and the herbs. Sauté until golden.

3. Add the water and stir to combine. Taste to adjust with herbs and spices.

3. Place lid on cooker, lock the PRESSURE SEAL, and bring up to pressure.

4. Once done, release pressure by quick release method.

5. Strain the liquid and save the solids for veggies cakes and burgers. Let the stock cool and place the liquid in jars for future use. It lasts 3 - 4 days in the fridge.

Mushroom Stock

This is the base of the mushroom barley soup. And it also goes great with risottos and as a substitute for the vegetable or beef stock. This broth blends well with fish and chicken, and could be easily upgraded into a soup with a potatoes or pasta. It's one of the best dishes to master your white wine deglazing skills.

Serves: 6 to 8
Preparation Time: 5 minutes
Cooking Time: 20 minutes

INGREDIENTS:

Salt and pepper to taste
Vegetable oil to taste
(2 tbsp) Rosemary, dry
(2 tbsp) Garlic, chopped
(1 cup) Onions, chopped

(1 cup) Celery, chopped
(1 cup) White wine, dry
(2 cups) Carrots, sliced
(2 cups) Mushroom, sliced
(4 cups) Water

COOKING STEPS:

1. Hit CANNING/PRESERVING followed by TIME ADJUSTMENT and correct time to 20 minutes.

2. Heat the oil and sauté the onion, the garlic and the mushrooms until brown. Season to taste.

3. Add remaining ingredients and stir to combine.

4. Place lid on cooker, lock the PRESSURE SEAL, and bring up to pressure.

5. Once done, release pressure by quick release method.

6. Strain the liquid and discard the solids. Let the stock cool and place the liquid in jars for future use. It lasts 3 - 4 days in the fridge and up to 6 months in the freezer.

Chicken Wing Stock

The most abundant, cheap and famous chicken cut, here makes a comeback as a no-time-to-lose golden broth. Great filler for sauces, soups and, well, almost every dish that needs water. It should cook under high-pressure until the meat falls easily off the bones. It lasts 2 to 3 days in the fridge and a lifetime in the mind of those who taste it.

Serves: 5 cups
Preparation Time: 10 minutes
Cooking Time: 40 minutes

INGREDIENTS:

Salt and pepper to taste
(1 tbsp) Thyme
(1 cup) Carrots, chopped
(1 cup) Celery, chopped

(1 cup) Onions, chopped
(6 cups) Water
(3 lbs) Chicken wings

COOKING STEPS:

1. Hit CANNING/PRESERVING and set time to 40 minutes.

2. Heat the oil in the pot. Add all the vegetables, the chicken and the herbs. Sauté until golden.

3. Add the water and stir to combine. Taste to adjust with herbs and spices.

4. Place lid on cooker, lock the PRESSURE SEAL, and bring up to pressure.

5. Once done, release pressure by slow release method, letting the steam escape naturally.

6. Strain the liquid and discard the solids. Let the stock cool and place the liquid in jars for future use. It lasts 3 - 4 days in the fridge and up to 6 months in the freezer.

Beef Stock

Bring this delicious broth as a base for dark sauces. Use it instead of water and cook wild varieties of rice. It goes well with everything that asks for a meaty flavor or tone, like tomatoes and mushrooms. Always cook it to the bones. Don't be afraid of bringing the pot back to the machine and letting it cook for few more minutes until the broth is perfect.

Serves: 6 cups
Preparation Time: 10 minutes
Cooking Time: 40 minutes

INGREDIENTS:

Salt and pepper to taste
(1 tbsp) Thyme
(1 cup) Celery, chopped
(1 cup) Onions, chopped

(2 cups) Carrots, chopped
(8 cups) Water
(3 lbs) Beef marrow bones, whole

COOKING STEPS:

1. Hit CANNING/PRESERVING followed by TIME ADJUSTMENT and correct time to 40 minutes.

2. Heat the oil in the pot. Add all the vegetables and the herbs. Sauté until golden.

3. Add the beef and the water. Stir to combine and season to taste.

4. Place lid on cooker, lock the PRESSURE SEAL, and bring up to pressure.

5. Once done, release pressure by slow release method, letting the steam escape naturally.

6. Strain the liquid and discard the solids. Let the stock cool and place the liquid in jars for future use. It lasts 3 - 4 days in the fridge and up to 6 months in the freezer.

Classic Tomato Marinara

If you need to know one tomato sauce recipe, that's the one. What should take 4 hours cooking in the regular stovetop pot, here is done in 30 minutes. It's the perfect base for sauces and marinades. Cook it in bulk and use it through the week in diverse other dishes. And, of course, drop in some fresh basil and serve it with pasta and a top of fresh parmesan cheese. Easy.

Serves: 4 - 6
Preparation Time: 10 minutes
Cooking Time: 30 minutes

INGREDIENTS:

Salt and pepper to taste
Olive oil to taste
(1 tbsp) Oregano
(1 tbsp) Thyme

(4 tbsp) Garlic, chopped
(1 cup) Vegetable stock
(2 cups) Onions, chopped
(3 lbs) Fresh tomatoes, cored, peeled

COOKING STEPS:

1. Hit CANNING/PRESERVING followed by TIME ADJUSTMENT and correct time to 30 minutes.

2. Heat the oil and sauté the tomatoes, the onions, the garlic and the herbs to soft and golden.

3. Add the tomatoes. Stir to combine. Sauté until the tomatoes boil up and get a bit lumpy.

4. Pour in the stock. Stir to combine. Season to taste.

5. Place lid on cooker, lock the PRESSURE SEAL, and bring up to pressure.

6. Once done, release pressure by slow release method, letting the steam escape naturally.

7. Let the sauce cool and transfer to glass jars. Keep in the fridge for up to 6 or 7 days, or do some serious canning with it for a longer shelf life. Use it as classic base for sauces, pasta toppings and soups.

Ragu

A dish perfected by centuries, it's now your time to bring it to life. Cook it deliciously for 20 minutes until the juicy pork gets combined with the tomato in a thick and rich sauce. The pasta holds everything together as the parmesan cheese tops it at the end. A dish that could save marriages.

Serves: 4 - 5
Preparation Time: 10 minutes
Cooking Time: 20 minutes

INGREDIENTS:

Salt and pepper to taste
Olive oil to taste
(1 tbsp) Thyme, dry
(1 tbsp) Oregano, dry
(2 tbsp) Garlic, chopped

(½ cup) Dry red wine
(2 cups) Onions, diced
(3 ½ cups) Tomato marinara sauce
(1 ½ lb) Pork ribs, ground

COOKING STEPS:

1. Hit CANNING/PRESERVING followed by TIME ADJUSTMENT and correct time to 20 minutes.

2. Heat the oil, add the garlic, the onions, the pork and the herbs. Season to taste. Gently pour in red wine for deglazing. Sauté until brown.

3. Add tomato sauce and stir to combine.

4. Place lid on cooker, lock the PRESSURE SEAL, and bring up to pressure.

5. Once done, release pressure by quick release method.

6. Stir to combine. Serve over cooked pasta and top with parmesan cheese.

Hot Pepper Sauce

You know you became a grown-up adult when you can make your own hot pepper sauce. Here we mixed the simplest recipes in a easy to follow base sauce for you to shine. Add your favorite spices, herbs and create your own secret homemade family sauce.

Serves: 4 - 5
Preparation Time: 1 minute
Cooking Time: 4 minutes

INGREDIENTS:

Salt and pepper to taste
Olive oil to taste
Herbs to taste

(1 cup) Vegetable stock
(2 cups) Apple cider vinegar
(3 cups) Sweet chili peppers

COOKING STEPS:

1. Add the peppers, the herbs, the stock and the vinegar to pot. Stir to combine. Season to taste.

2. Hit FISH/VEG/STEAM followed by TIME ADJUSTMENT and correct time to 4 minutes.

4. Place lid on cooker, lock the PRESSURE SEAL, and bring up to pressure.

5. Once done, release pressure by quick release method.

6. Stir to combine. Let it cool down, bring to small bowl or bottles and serve as dip for meals and snacks.

Sweet-Sour Sauce

Sugar, pineapple and vinegar. This bombastic explosion of tastes made Asian kitchen famous all over the world. Here you learn how to do it yourself in only 4 minutes. Cook it to perfection and serve it along every type of dish or snack.

Serves: 4
Preparation Time: 10 minutes
Cooking Time: 4 minutes

INGREDIENTS:

Salt and pepper to taste
Flour (wheat, corn) to thicken
(1 cup) Brown sugar

(1 cup) White wine vinegar
(3 cups) Pineapple juice

COOKING STEPS:

1. Hit FISH/VEG/STEAM followed by TIME ADJUSTMENT and correct time to 4 minutes.

2. Add every ingredient to the pot and stir to combine. Season to taste.

3. Place lid on cooker, lock the PRESSURE SEAL, and bring up to pressure.

4. Once done, release pressure by quick release method.

5. Stir to combine. Add more flour to thicken the sauce. Let it cool down, bring to a small bowl and serve as dip for meals and snacks.

Peanut Sauce

You can make your own peanut butter fast under high-pressure. Turn it into a sauce with a blender and it's ready to be served. Add it to grilled chicken and you get Thai satay. It goes great also with salads and snacks.

Serves: 4
Preparation Time: 3 minutes
Cooking Time: 25 minutes

INGREDIENTS:

Salt and pepper to taste
(1 tbsp) Ginger, minced
(2 tbsp) Soy sauce

(4 cups) Peanut, dry, peeled, unsalted
(5 cups) Water

COOKING STEPS:

1. Add the water and the peanut to the pot.

2. Hit CANNING/PRESERVING followed by TIME ADJUSTMENT and correct time to 25 minutes.

3. Place lid on cooker, lock the PRESSURE SEAL, and bring up to pressure.

4. Once done, release pressure by quick release method.

5. Bring peanuts to blender or food processor and reduce it to a cream. Add remaining ingredients and blend to combine. Season to taste. Bring peanut sauce to small bowls and serve as a dip for snacks and meals.

BBQ Sauce

A great base for marinating meats, this sauce can easily become a family favorite. Bring it to the life with fresh ingredients to create a sauce worth of its own bottle and label. Add your favorite spices and herbs, and surprise friends with your very homemade BBQ sauce.

Serves: 4
Preparation Time: 5 minutes
Cooking Time: 10 minutes

INGREDIENTS:

Salt and pepper to taste
Vegetable oil to taste
(1 tbsp) Liquid smoke essence
(1 tbsp) Garlic, minced
(2 tbsp) Honey

(2 tbsp) Red wine vinegar
(½ cup) Beef stock
(1 cup) Onion, chopped
(2 cups) Tomato sauce

COOKING STEPS:

1. Hit SOUP/STEW and set time to default (10 minutes).

2. Heat the oil, add the garlic and onions to the pot. Sauté until brown.

3. Add remaining ingredients and stir to combine. Season to taste.

4. Place lid on cooker, lock the PRESSURE SEAL, and bring up to pressure.

5. Once done, release pressure by quick release method.

6. Stir to combine. Bring sauce to small bowls and serve along dips, snacks and sandwiches.

Join Our FREE Cookbook Club

Why should you join?

- ⊘ Get new books we publish for free
- ⊘ Get huge discounts on new products we promote
- ⊘ Get recipes, secrets and techniques straight from the pros to your inbox
- ⊘ Get access to our convenient kitchen guides

SIGN UP AT COOKINGWITHAFOODIE.COM

Made in the USA
San Bernardino, CA
23 October 2016